British science fiction writer, editor and critic Graham Sleight is editor of *Foundation: The International Review of Science Fiction.*

GRAHAM SLEIGHT

THE DOCTOR'S MONSTERS

MEANINGS OF THE MONSTROUS IN *DOCTOR WHO*

I.B. TAURIS

LONDON · NEW YORK

Published in 2012 by I.B.Tauris & Co Ltd
6 Salem Road, London W2 4BU
175 Fifth Avenue, New York NY 10010
www.ibtauris.com

Distributed in the United States and Canada
Exclusively by Palgrave Macmillan
175 Fifth Avenue, New York, NY 10010

ISBN: 978 1 84885 178 8

A full CIP record for this book is available from the British Library
A full CIP record is available from the Library of Congress

Library of Congress Catalog Card Number: available

Printed and bound in Sweden by ScandBook AB

To my grandfather, Ronald Curtiss,
who built Daleks

CONTENTS

FOREWORD

The original use of the word 'monster' is something close to what my friend, the great science fiction academic and historian Graham Sleight, has at the centre of his thesis in this book: to be a monster is to be excessive, too much of something, a tumour in the body of nature. Our hunter/gatherer ancestors might have landed a 'monster' fish or run from a 'monster' boar. Or at least the stories they told when they got back to the campfire would insist on those monsters.

But if there's one thing a small child loves, it's too much of something. Something unmoderated, unconfined, a trait running free, unencumbered by society, able to stay up as late as it likes and eat all the ice cream. No wonder children love the Daleks: it's them, in armour and in charge.

But a Dalek is also, of course, a Nazi in a tank.

So a Dalek is at least two things, and those things, encompassing love and hate as they do, might be seen as opposites being forced together. It's a threat to home comforts that literally includes its audience. That fusion may be where the Dalek's archetypal power comes from.

The Doctor, indeed, seems to wander the universe with an eye on both those poles, saying that he'll shake the hand of anything with a different body shape, but usually ending up exterminating 'the other'. The show in its modern incarnation has remarked on this at length. As Steven Moffat says of his hero, 'Nice guy, if you're a biped.'

Unpacking meaning in that way is the job Graham has set himself. And he's picked a great playground. The monsters of *Doctor Who* are often where the show's meanings come to the surface, just as the tales of those hunter/gatherers must have said a lot about them. In here, you'll find meanings psychological, social and political, sometimes consciously expressed, sometimes revealing of impulse and reflex, sometimes the work of one creator, sometimes something built by many over time, and thus reflecting a changing world like nothing else could.

Works like this often get a rough ride from fandom, as evidenced by comments on *io9* articles and reviews in *SFX*. It still comes as a shock to me that an audience that's meant to be ready to embrace the future and the alien, when encountering the everyday vocabulary of critical thought, sometimes doesn't reach for the dictionary, but instead pillories the author for making them feel stupid. Well, it's the duty of any author to point to the truth. But *Doctor Who* fandom also likes to *celebrate* the intellectual, and Graham meets the fan community halfway, with a text that's mostly written in the vernacular, and reaches the other way too, offering, incidentally, a splendid introduction to the vast worlds of *Doctor Who* for those engaged in the critical study of SF. I think his analysis makes old stories exciting again, finding new interest even in such oddities as the Borad.

The Doctor's Monsters makes a splendid contribution to academia, pop culture and fan pub debate. I heartily recommend it.

Paul Cornell
Buckinghamshire

ACKNOWLEDGEMENTS

My first debt is to Roz Kaveney, author of *Superheroes* among many other books. She was generous enough to suggest that Philippa Brewster of I.B.Tauris approach me to write this book. Philippa has been enormously encouraging to a first-time author, as has the rest of the team at I.B.Tauris. In particular, I'm enormously grateful to her for remaining calm when a broken leg put back my schedule for completing this book by several months. Roz provided wise advice down the phone on many evenings.

A number of friends offered specifically *Who*-related expertise: Jonathan Clements, Rose Fox, Simon Guerrier, Luke Gutzwiller, Iain Harris, Tony Keen, Victoria McManus, and Tim Phipps. Others provided hospitality, encouragement, support, distraction or food: Tom Anderson, Liz Batty, Chris Barzak, Amelia Beamer, Simon Bradshaw, the late Charles N Brown, Nicola Clarke, John Clute, Judith Clute, Liz Hand, Roger Hart, Niall Harrison, Dan Hartland, Andrew Hogg, Alex Ingram, Josh Jasper, Giles Lewis, Tim Lewis, Martin Lewis, Kevin Maroney, Farah Mendlesohn, Chance Morrison, Abigail Nussbaum, Anna Raftery, Jon Reades, Jonathan Strahan, Liza Groen Trombi, Hester Wells, and Gary Wolfe. Noted without comment is Tim Lewis's proposal that this book be titled *Let Zygons Be Zygons*.

Paul Cornell offered to write a Foreword almost before I'd finished telling him about the book, and I know I'm not the only one to have benefited from his support and encouragement.

Some of the ideas present here were first aired, in different forms, in papers given at Readercon and the International Conference on the Fantastic in the Arts over the last few years. I'm grateful to the organisers of these events for creating an environment that has felt good to talk in.

A series of indulgent bosses and colleagues have not looked askance at my extra-curricular activities, and even encouraged them: I want particularly to mention Jo Ball, Mary Butler, Brian Dow, Chris Hanvey, Michael Moskowitz, Mike Poole, Yasir Musawar, Sarah Quinlan, Olly Rice, Cesare Sacerdoti, Susan Scott, Malcolm Smith and Len Tyler. I'm very glad that Klara and Eric King's work on the index renews an old connection. I would like to thank the team at Newgen Knowledge Works, Chennai, for all their help with the production of this book.

My family has put up with me for longer than most, and I hope this finally answers the question of why I need so many books. To my father, my mother, Chris and Alison, my thanks and love.

Westerners are all unconscious Manicheans; perhaps most people everywhere are. One has only to remember the common reaction to Eichmann's trial ('a fiend in human form' as if the soul and the crimes must somehow match in essence), or the usual reactions of people to political opponents, to see that most of us believe – somewhere, somehow – that Evil and Good both have a substantive being apart from the historically accidental, particular acts that people do. Good and Evil are conceived as nouns, not adjectives.

> – Joanna Russ, 1968 review of James Blish's *Black Easter*, collected in *The Country You Have Never Seen* (2007)

The Master's voice was cool. 'That is a demonstration of the causal nexus, Monitor. The electro-muscular constrictor gives me complete control over that hand. Please replace the screen, Doctor. Or one of your young friends will eliminate the other.'

The Doctor had no choice. Seeing him forced to do as the Master demanded, Tegan's anger boiled over. 'You revolting man. I wouldn't take orders from you if you were the last man in the universe.'

'Which he may well be, if he carries on like this,' said the Doctor when the screen was in place again. 'Don't you see what the Monitor is telling us, Master? Logopolis isn't the academic backwater it seems, but somehow crucial to the structure of creation.'

'I have never been susceptible to argument based on abstract nouns, Doctor.'

> – Christopher H Bidmead, *Doctor Who: Logopolis* (1982)

INTRODUCTION

The premise of this book is that the monstrous stands for something, and that it's worth making explicit what that something is. More specifically, it often makes sense to consider something monstrous as the personification of one human trait to the exclusion of all others, and so as a cautionary tale about the dangers of that trait. The monster, in fact, may be an embodiment and a literalisation of that trait; it can play out in how the monster looks, how it behaves and how it's defeated. (Monsters almost always are defeated in stories. Normality winds up reasserting itself, perhaps at a cost.)

The source from which I'm going to draw my examples is the BBC television programme *Doctor Who*, which has run from 1963 to the present. Monsters have, of course, long been one of the main features – one of the selling points – of the show. They provide, especially for its younger viewers, a shiver of terror, and perhaps the delight of watching 'from behind the sofa'. (For more on what viewers get out of the programme, see Tulloch and Jenkins's *Science Fiction Audiences* [1995].) Although I assume most readers will be familiar with the various phases of the show's development, I provide an overview below in 'A brief history of *Doctor Who*'.

In a sense, my argument takes off from a remark by the late scientist Jakob Bronowski in his TV series *The Ascent of Man* (1973). Bronowski said that what distinguished *homo sapiens* from most animals is that we're not niche creatures. A polar bear, a crocodile and a lion are shaped by evolutionary forces to fit their environment by 'exact and beautiful adaptations by which an animal fits into its environment like one cog-wheel into another'. But evolution 'has not fitted man to any specific environment. On the contrary, by comparison with [other animals] he has a rather crude survival kit. And yet – this is the paradox of the human condition – one that fits him to all environments'.

I want to argue that the opposite is true of most *Doctor Who* monsters. That is, they're shaped into very specific forms by external pressures, and so they are *narrower* in their natures than humans are. The Daleks, for instance, are mutated forms of an originally humanoid species, the Kaleds, further altered by genetic manipulation, and then placed into metal travel machines designed to support them. They are depicted as physically and therefore morally limited creatures. The Cybermen are narrower because they've had all their emotions stripped away. The Sontarans are only concerned with war, the Wirrn with finding new homes and new hosts; and so on.

Further, I want to suggest that this narrowness is in very visible contrast to the values espoused by the Doctor and other identification figures in the story. Because they lack the adaptive flexibility of humans, monsters can be trapped into narrow (and so defeatable) behaviours; very often humanity is portrayed as 'better than' monsters as a result. There's a sense, then, in which the portrayal of monsters in *Doctor Who* can often be taken as a kind of moral parable: the Doctor opposes not merely the monsters themselves, but the values they represent. As I'll suggest, *Doctor Who* often comes down to an argument between competing systems of values. This is hardly unique among stories in general, of course, but the span of the programme does give us a chance to look at how the same questions (like 'the worth of the emotions' with the Cybermen) are treated in a wide range of contexts.

This kind of argument has a number of potential problems, which I should address briefly. The first is the question of whether what I'm seeing in the television programmes is 'really' there or just something I'm imposing on them. Claiming that it's possible to divine perfectly the author's intention, and that this intention matters above other inter-pretations, has long been thought of as 'the intentional fal-lacy' in literary criticism, and I don't need to rehearse here why it's a trap. Indeed, it's even more of a trap when consid-ering a television series which is, by its nature, a collabora-tive enterprise. Simply because a given feature appears in a story with a certain writer's name on it doesn't mean that the named writer is responsible. It might be a director's or actor's addition to a script – and that's leaving aside the often thorny issue of how much a given piece of *Doctor Who* is written by the named writer and how much by the script editor or other member of the production team.

On the other hand, though, as long as one accepts that authorial intention is one narrative among many, I see no problem with accepting it as such. One of the benefits of studying *Doctor Who*, as opposed to almost any other TV ser-ies, is that fan scholarship has so extensively documented the production process. It would be silly to disregard the stated views of the series' creators as recorded in interviews, DVD commentaries and the like – so long as one remembers that their views are only one account, and that they may (like any-one else) self-censor, unconsciously omit or simply not see a particular meaning in what they've helped to create.

So it is valid, I'd suggest, to cite what an author or an actor may have said about a given story. It's not always necessary to agree with the authors, though – the memory can cheat, they may have their own agenda, and so on. The readings I arrive at are, I hope, based on as much evidence as pos-sible including, but not limited to, what was intended at the outset.

The second risk is overinterpretation. *Doctor Who* has been, and continues to be, a series made under great pressure and one that stretches everyone involved with it; see, for instance, Davies and Cook (2008). It's always a risk that the critic or viewer will assign great significance to a detail that results from one of the contingencies of production. A certain detail might not be intended to bear great meaning, but might sim-ply be what was possible at the time, what felt right in a 3am rewrite or what could be got away with. My quotation from

Christopher Bidmead's *Logopolis* novelisation at the start of the book is meant to serve as a warning to myself (or anyone else) not to get too far from the shows themselves into the terrain where abstract nouns are detached from what they denote.

The last risk is, to be blunt, taking *Doctor Who* too seriously. Many will object, I'm sure, that the show is 'a children's show' or 'just entertainment', that the kind of scrutiny and interpretation I'm bringing to bear on it isn't appropriate. That may in the end just be a matter of personal preference. I suppose my starting point is that if something's worth enjoying, it's also worth thinking about. What was it that made it enjoyable? What does it say about me that I enjoyed it? I certainly don't share the idea that just because *Doctor Who* is (partly) aimed at younger viewers, it's less worthy of serious attention than something solely for adults. But equally, I have to recognise that *Doctor Who* is a show primarily aimed to get a family audience watching together. It doesn't often plumb existential depths, it excludes large areas of human experience and it often takes short cuts in its depiction of character and motivation. *Doctor Who* may not be only entertainment, but it does have to be entertainment first. I'm also conscious that, while of course my efforts aren't in the same class, similar thoughts have been put forward about other kinds of stories, for instance, Bruno Bettelheim's famous book *The Uses of Enchantment* on the deeper meanings of fairy tales. JRR Tolkien's famous lecture 'Beowulf: The Monsters and the Critics' (1936) addresses many of the same issues I'm wanting to, in particular in its assertion that the monsters in the Beowulf story are at least as interesting as the human characters. Similarly, it's not a new idea to assert that fantastic creatures embody one particular trait. That's famously true of the deities in many pantheistic religions, such as the Greek gods described in Graves (1955).

It's worth saying that the subject of monstrousness has been considered from various angles by other authors, both in the context of *Doctor Who*, and more generally. I differ from an author like David J Howe (1997) in not focussing especially on the production process that gave rise to a particular monster. My concern, instead, is with the way a monster is presented onscreen. As a consequence of this, I'm particularly interested in how a monster's nature is progressively revealed. We very rarely find out the whole truth about a monster in one go. Instead, a typical *Doctor Who* story will be an incremental process of discovery about an environment or a monster. (As Jakob Bronowski would argue, the two are often closely related.) This process of discovery is especially important in stories like *The Claws of Axos* (Chapter 6) or *Full Circle* (Chapter 20), in which the Doctor's role as a scientist is foregrounded. But, to a greater or lesser extent, he's always a scientist, always an enquirer, observer and discoverer. So it matters how the process of discovery is worked out and presented.

The question arises of what a monster is. A rough definition would be that it's a creature of nonhuman appearance that acts in a way that's evil, or at least to harm the protagonist and other characters we're meant to be sympathetic with. That may sound a little circular, but there's rarely any ambiguity in *Doctor Who* about who's on the side of good. The Doctor's companions may be tempted towards evil (as Tegan is by the Mara, see Chapter 31), and the Doctor himself may appear to be acting in a self-centred way (as he does in *The Invasion of Time*, see Chapter 9). But these occurrences are marked out by their extreme rarity. It's far more common for the Doctor, his companions and those characters they trust to be the stable point in a story. The monsters, then, are the creatures that oppose 'our' characters.

This definition excludes a number of creatures that might be considered as monsters. The Draconians, for instance, in *Frontier in Space* (1973), are a nonhuman race of very distinctive appearance. But they're no more evil than the humans who oppose them in their long-running cold war. The Master is certainly monstrous in his various deeds, and he has appeared in disfigured form in *The Deadly Assassin* (1976) and *The Keeper of Traken* (1981). But he primarily has, and indeed capitalises on, a human form. So monsters for the purpose of this book are creatures that act in an evil way and look in some fashion abnormal.

A book of this scale can't be comprehensive, and I'm conscious that I won't be able to cover everyone's favourite creatures. As an example, anecdotally, there's one question that *Doctor Who* fans are asked about the series more than any other: Which was the story with the giant maggots in it? The answer is that it was *The Green Death* (1973), a tale about a chemicals company opening up a plant in Wales and, through the dumping of its pollutants down an old mineshaft, creating mutations such as the giant maggots. It's a prime example of the way the series has embedded itself in the British collective consciousness. *The Green Death* has many other memorable things about it: a mad computer behind the scenes, a topical ecological theme and the emotional departure of the Doctor's companion Jo Grant. So why is it that the maggots are so memorable? For a start, it might be that maggots give almost anyone a queasy feeling in their natural form. They're associated with death, with eating the flesh of corpses and other such unwholesome ideas. It might also be that, unlike some creatures in *Doctor Who*, the maggots are pretty well realised. Some long-shots of them aren't entirely convincing, but in close up, they're as skin-crawling to look at as you'd expect. As creatures to interact with, though, they're pretty boring. They don't talk, they don't reason, they can't argue a case in words as some monsters can. All they can do is provide a threat, an opportunity to put characters in jeopardy. They're not even the prime movers of the story; they're just a function of the other, real threat, the chemicals plant's pollution.

The same argument could be made about some of the series' other famous monsters, such as the Yeti. These creatures, which appeared in *The Abominable Snowmen*+ (1967) and *The Web of Fear*+ (1968) are robots in the shape of the legendary abominable snowman of the Himalayas. They are tall, ferocious and have various ways of killing people. But they're also without speech, and ultimately controlled by an entity known as The Great Intelligence. In both stories, the

+ As noted below, this symbol denotes that a given story is only partly preserved in the BBC archives.

Doctor's fight is not with these creatures, but with the entity that's using them.

One similar creature is the one that I'm going to consider in the first chapter, the Autons. They too are just puppets of a controlling force. But the Autons are more interesting than the Yeti, I think, because of how they're tied in to contemporary anxieties. In any case, I hope that the following chapters provide an informative survey both of the monsters that have enlivened *Doctor Who* and what, perhaps, they mean. Along the way, I hope also that I'll provide a history – from an unusual angle – of how this most enduring of TV science fiction series has created and recreated itself.

A BRIEF HISTORY OF
DOCTOR WHO

*D*octor Who emerged from a series of discussions within the BBC in the early 1960s about producing a science fiction series. Under the aegis of head of drama Sydney Newman, producer Verity Lambert and script editor David Whitaker, a basic format for the series was hammered out. The programme was first broadcast on 23 November 1963, the day after the assassination of John F Kennedy. Its first, four-episode story, *An Unearthly Child*, begins from the viewpoint of two teachers in a contemporary London school. One of their pupils, Susan Foreman, is displaying knowledge that seems not just unusual for her age but which contradicts established scientific and historical fact. Made curious – also by Susan's references to being looked after by her grandfather – they follow her home one night to the address she has given, which turns out to be a junkyard. There they meet the Doctor, a mysterious old man played by William Hartnell. He seems to be concealing something, and the teachers hear Susan's voice coming from a police box in the junkyard. Stumbling into it, they find it is vastly bigger on the inside than the outside, filled with bizarre technological equipment. Susan and the Doctor explain that it is called the TARDIS, and that it has been their home while they have been 'wanderers in the fourth dimension'. Now that they have been found out, they will need to move on. The two teachers, still disbelieving, watch as the Doctor activates the TARDIS' controls and so takes it to another time and place. When the travellers look out of the door again, they have landed on prehistoric Earth, where most of the action of *An Unearthly Child* takes place.

The series' popularity was cemented by its second story, *The Daleks* (1963–64), which introduced the Doctor's most famous adversaries; see Chapter 7 for more discussion of this story. The immense popular success of the Daleks guaranteed their return (in *The Dalek Invasion of Earth* [1964], also the first story to see one of the Doctor's travelling companions depart). Slowly, a stable format was established: about 40 25-minute episodes of the series were broadcast each year, divided up into separate serials. In some cases, the TARDIS would land in Earth's past. In the early years, these 'historicals', such as *The Aztecs* (1964), would have no science-fictional content, and were seen as part of the programme's educational function. The majority of stories, though, were set in the future, often on alien worlds; the extreme case is *The Web Planet* (1965), which featured no human characters apart from the Doctor and his companions. At this stage, the commonest trope of the series' later years – contemporary Earth under threat, usually from alien invaders – was hardly seen at all, although stories such as *The War Machines* (1966) and *The Tenth Planet*+ (1966) began to head in that direction.

Hartnell continued in the role of the Doctor for just over three years, though his increasing ill health and irascibility caused problems for the production team. With the arrival of a new producer, Innes Lloyd, the decision was taken to replace him, but continue the programme. At the end of *The Tenth Planet* (1966), after complaining of 'tiredness', the Doctor collapsed and changed his shape entirely into a new one; he was now played by the character actor Patrick Troughton. Troughton also held the role for three years, but in his era, the series edged much closer to its present shape. Firstly, the 'pure' historical stories all but ended. (Apart from *Black Orchid* [1982], the last of these was *The Highlanders*+ (1966–67), Troughton's second story.) Secondly, the contemporary-Earth-under-threat stories became more prominent. In particular, *The Web of Fear*+ (1968) and *The Invasion*+ (1968) represent first attempts at doing such stories in a large-scale way. The latter introduces UNIT, the United Nations Intelligence Taskforce, a military body concerned with defending the planet from alien invasion. Up to this point, the Doctor's origins had remained vague. It was clear that he was not human, on the run from his own people and that there existed at least one other such renegade (the Meddling Monk from *The Time Meddler* [1965]). But not much more had been revealed until Troughton's last story, *The War Games* (1969). Here, the Doctor encounters a threat that he feels is too great to deal with on his own and so he is forced to summon his own people, the Time Lords, to help. Although they solve the problem – they are depicted as almost omnipotent – they also put the Doctor on trial for his interference in the existence of other worlds, an act against their code. The Doctor makes the argument that he always interferes in order to defeat evil, and this appears to be heard sympathetically. But in the end he is found guilty and sentence pronounced: He is to be exiled to Earth, be stripped of his knowledge of time travel and have his appearance changed.

Accordingly, in the next story, Troughton was succeeded as the Doctor by Jon Pertwee. Pertwee's era brought several changes. Firstly, from his debut story *Spearhead from Space* (1970), the series was broadcast in colour. Secondly, the length of each series was shortened from 40 or so episodes to about 25. This made the pressures on the production team less intense, and so allowed more elaborate programme-making. Lastly, for several years, the Earthbound Doctor became a semi-official 'scientific adviser' to UNIT, while trying to repair his TARDIS and regain the freedom he so valued. This situation changed from *The Three Doctors* (1973), in which the Doctor, in collaboration with his two earlier selves, saved the universe from a truly devastating threat posed by Omega, one of the founders of the Time Lord race. The Pertwee years also saw the introduction of the Master, a villain explicitly designed to be Moriarty to the Doctor's Holmes: a fellow Time Lord who was a worthy (and returning) adversary. However, the actor who played him, Roger Delgado, died in a car crash in 1973, and so the prospect of a final showdown between him and Pertwee's Doctor was lost.

By the time Pertwee stepped down, after five years in the role, the programme was cemented in the popular imagination (at least in the UK) as an immutable part of Saturday night television. The casting process for Pertwee's replacement seems to have been more than usually protracted, but the production team eventually settled on a relatively unknown actor, Tom Baker. So began the era which, for its length if nothing else, has most defined the programme. Baker held the role for seven years, a record still unequalled. The first three years of this period, under producer/script editor team Philip Hinchcliffe and Robert Holmes, are often labelled 'gothic'. The show went further than before or since into the territory of horror, gleefully ransacking myths like the Frankenstein story. Another high point of the Hinchcliffe years was *The Deadly Assassin* (1976), a Holmes-written story that debunked the Time Lord mythos and presented them as an ossified and conservative society that had lost touch with the roots of its power. It was easy to see why the Doctor (and the Master) would have fled such a place. But the Hinchcliffe/Holmes approach drew criticism, especially from Mary Whitehouse and her National Viewers' and Listeners' Association, which took particular exception to some of the violence in *The Deadly Assassin*. Hinchcliffe stepped down in 1977 and was replaced by Graham Williams, who was given an explicit brief to bring humour to the fore instead of horror. Williams certainly fulfilled this assignment, particularly in the 1979–80 season which had Douglas Adams, author of *The Hitch-Hiker's Guide to the Galaxy*, as script editor. Williams' time on the series has been criticised, for making stories too 'silly' and for allowing the programme to become increasingly a vehicle for Baker's florid and irresistible charisma. But it was certainly a period of ratings success, including (in *City of Death* [1979]) an all-time high UK viewership of 16.1 million.

A turning-point was reached with the arrival of John Nathan-Turner as producer in 1980. The reign of JN-T, as he became known – he had a flair for self-publicity – lasted until the show's cancellation in 1989, and no figure in the series' history generates more polarised opinions. Nathan-Turner's first season as producer was also Baker's last, and it was an unusually sombre affair, also marked by relatively low ratings. Baker was replaced in the lead by Peter Davison, up to that point best known as playing the vet Tristan Farnon on the BBC's series *All Creatures Great and Small*. Davison's and Nathan-Turner's stated aim was to make the Doctor more vulnerable, and Davison's three years certainly achieved this, most notably when, in the story *Earthshock* (1982), one of the Doctor's travelling companions was killed. Although Davison never attempted to emulate the grandiosity of some of his predecessors, his performance was, along with Troughton's, perhaps the finest piece of acting in the role up to this point. His time in the role also saw the series shifted, for the first time ever, to broadcast on weekday evenings. This helped to avoid any further decline in ratings, and helped contribute to a sense that the old consensus of family television viewing together on Saturday evenings was no longer holding together.

When Davison announced his departure, Nathan-Turner fairly quickly settled on the actor Colin Baker as his successor. Baker's tenure in the role was, sadly, the most controversial to date. Halfway through his first full season as the Doctor in 1985, the Controller of BBC1, Michael Grade, announced that he was putting the series on 'hiatus' for 18 months. This clear vote of no confidence, bolstered by poor ratings for the season, led many to conclude that the series was past its best. When it returned, in 1986, it was only for 14 25-minute episodes, and the resulting story (*The Trial of a Time Lord*) was marked also by the departure of the series' script editor, Eric Saward. Saward compounded the show's problems by giving an interview to the magazine *Starburst* in which he was pointedly critical of Nathan-Turner's personality and approach. It's perhaps surprising that the series wasn't cancelled outright at this point, but Grade chose another course. He required that Baker leave the role, and recommissioned another 14-episode season.

Sylvester McCoy's three-year tenure as the Doctor was, in many respects, a disappointing one. Ratings continued to decline, the show was being visibly outpaced in special effects by what was offered in the cinemas and there was no sense – as there had been in the 1970s – that this series was a central part of the UK's cultural life. Yet there is much in this era to be treasured. Saward's replacement as script editor, Andrew Cartmel, gathered around him a group of largely young and untried writers, and produced some of the densest and most intricate scripts in the series' history. McCoy also grew into the role progressively, and the series slowly re-established the Doctor as a figure of mystery, a manipulator not altogether to be trusted. But it was to no avail; when the Doctor walked into the distance at the end of *Survival* (1989), and the series was finally taken off air, it seemed perfectly likely that it would not return to television.

After the cancellation, Doctor Who was kept alive in a number of ways. There was by this point a thriving fan culture centred on the series, not only in the UK but also in North America and Australia. A series of professionally published *New Adventures* novels continued from where *Survival* had left off, and the best of them made the Doctor's character very much more complex and ambiguous than it had ever been on television. These books also served as a testing ground for new writers such as Mark Gatiss and Paul Cornell, who would later go on to professional TV careers, and ultimately to write for the revived series. There were also audio adventures, in the first instance unofficially fan-produced, latterly officially endorsed and produced by the company Big Finish. And *Doctor Who Magazine*, founded as a weekly in 1979, subsequently became a monthly and has continued to document the series' history right up to the present day.

Through the early 1990s, there were a number of abortive attempts, both by the BBC and independent producers, to revive the show. These are ably chronicled in Jean-Marc and Randy Lofficer's *The Nth Doctor* (1997). Finally, one of these came to fruition, and resulted in the broadcast of a TV Movie, *Doctor Who* (1996), with Paul McGann in the lead. Although this performed well in the UK, it did not do so in North America, and so any chance of a continuing series following from it faded.

A further revival came in 2005, led by the long-time fan Russell T Davies. Davies had been a contributor to the *New Adventures*, had carved out a successful career for himself as a writer for TV, including his series *Queer as Folk* (1999–2000), featuring a gay *Doctor Who* fan. The revived first series of *Doctor Who*, comprising 13 45-minute episodes, broadcast on BBC1 on Saturday nights, was a huge success, not only in ratings terms, but also in the sense that it seemed to re-establish the tradition of communal family viewing that had been lost in the digital multichannel world since 1989. The ninth Doctor (in the 2005 series) was played by the experienced actor Christopher Eccleston; his successor, David Tennant, was somewhat younger but no less popular. Davies eventually supervised four full series from 2005–8, plus a clutch of specials broadcast in 2009. The last of these, broadcast at Christmas 2009, saw David Tennant's regeneration into the 11th Doctor, Matt Smith. As I write in October 2011, Smith's second season has just completed its transmission. Smith's reign has been overseen by Davies' chosen successor, Steven Moffat, one of the most popular writers during Davies' era. The show has also spawned two spin-offs, *The Sarah Jane Adventures*, for younger viewers, and *Torchwood*, for older ones. It seems now to be one of the most important brands that the BBC wishes to preserve. Indeed, at this point, it hardly seems appropriate to speak of *Doctor Who* as solely or even mainly as a TV programme. It exists also as a website containing downloadable interactive adventures, books, CDs, DVDs, exhibitions, theatre productions and it is even represented in concerts in the BBC's venerable Proms series. For the moment, at least, the show's future seems secure.

As will be apparent from this narrative, there's a penumbra of *Doctor Who* stories around the core of those that have been broadcast on television. There are books, audio adventures and fan productions of various kinds. Indeed, as the digital age has made the tools for filming and editing more accessible than ever, it's never been easier for a sufficiently interested *Doctor Who* watcher to create, in some form or other, his or her own story. This book restricts itself almost entirely to the adventures broadcast as part of the TV series.

There are plenty of reasons for this, but the most obvious one is sheer scope. Even by concentrating just on the TV series, I have a potential 200 stories and more than 780 episodes to consider. The second is a sense in which the TV series represents the official 'canon' of *Doctor Who*, or its core reality whereas stories told in other media are not always taken as so definitive.

A glance at the contents list will also make clear that this book jumps about in the series' chronology, and does not attempt to provide a full reference to all monsters featured in the series. Although I provide a Glossary which does aim for some degree of comprehensiveness, I'm all too aware that there are such reference books available already offering A–Z listings of all the entities in the series.

A NOTE ON USAGE

A significant proportion of the *Doctor Who* stories broadcast before 1970 no longer exist in the BBC archives. Purges of 'unwanted' material in the 1960s and 1970s mean that 106 of the episodes featuring William Hartnell and Patrick Troughton as the Doctor are no longer held by the BBC. Nonetheless, audio recordings of all stories exist, and for many there are 'telesnaps' – that is, off-air photographs, both usually taken by fans. These telesnaps have in some cases been combined with the surviving audio to create fan-made reconstructions of missing episodes.

In this book, when I refer to a story for which all of the original episodes are missing, its title is followed on first appearance by an asterisk: *The Power of the Daleks*+ (1966). When some but not all of the episodes are missing, the title is followed on first appearance by a plus sign: *The Ice Warriors*+ (1967). The archival purges that resulted in this loss also mean that a few episodes from the Jon Pertwee era only exist in black and white rather than the original colour, though colour can sometimes be restored to these episodes, as in the recent DVD release of *Planet of the Daleks* (1973).

All stories up to *The Gunfighters* (1966) did not have, on broadcast, individual titles. Rather, a four-episode story such as this had individual episodes titled, in this case, 'A Holiday for the Doctor', 'Don't Shoot the Pianist', 'Johnny Ringo', and 'The OK Corral'. In a couple of cases, most obviously *The Daleks* (1963–64), variant titles exist. This story was known for many years as 'The Dead Planet', after the first of its seven episodes. I take as canonical those titles used on BBC VHS and DVD releases and, in the cases in which there has been no such release, those used in the BBC book *Doctor Who: The Television Companion* (Howe and Walker, 1998).

Some stories in the new (post-2005) series comprise two or three episodes; because no clear title has been accepted as canonical for these stories, I refer to them by episode titles, such as *Bad Wolf/The Parting of the Ways* (2005).

I date stories according to their time of first broadcast on BBC television in the UK. Accordingly, some of them have dates spanning two years, such as *The Daleks* (1963–64), broadcast in seven episodes between December 1963 and February 1964.

THE AUTONS
(1970, 1971, 2005, 2010)

Twice now, the same image has been used to relaunch *Doctor Who*. A high street in contemporary Britain, populated with shoppers and familiar stores, is filled with the sound of breaking glass. The shop-window dummies have begun to come to life and are breaking out of their displays. Jerkily but relentlessly, they follow the shoppers. Their hands fall away to reveal guns of some alien design. The guns fire and pedestrians collapse in clouds of smoke. Mayhem ensues.

This image, found in both *Spearhead from Space* (1970) and *Rose* (2005) is so obviously arresting that it's easy to see why writers and producers have lighted on it as a narrative hook. The creatures concerned, the Autons, are described as being made of 'living plastic', and under the control of an alien intelligence known as the Nestene Consciousness. In their one other major appearance, *Terror of the Autons* (1971), the shop-window dummies are not used, but other plastic creations are.

Spearhead from Space was made at a crucial time in *Doctor Who*'s development. It was the first story of Jon Pertwee's tenure as the Doctor, the first to be made in colour and the first to showcase the series' new format of being predominantly set on Earth. It was written by Robert Holmes, a writer who had first worked for the series in the previous season, Patrick Troughton's last as the Doctor. Neither of his stories there, *The Space Pirates*+ (1969) and *The Krotons* (1969), were terribly distinguished, but it seems that the production office formed a high opinion of his skills as a result of them. Through the accident of an industrial dispute, *Spearhead from Space* became the first *Doctor Who* story to be shot entirely on location film, a happy accident that lent cinema-verite vividness to several sequences, not least of them being the dummies' attack.

The story begins quietly enough: A ground-based observation station spots a group of meteors falling to earth in a spearhead formation. At about the same time, the TARDIS lands in some woods and the Doctor falls out of its open door. He is soon found and taken to hospital, while one of the meteors – a plastic sphere about a foot wide – is recovered from its crater by Seeley, a poacher. At the hospital, the Doctor is taken under the protection of Brigadier Lethbridge-Stewart of the United Nations Intelligence Taskforce (UNIT). Lethbridge-Stewart recognises the TARDIS from past encounters with the Doctor, but not the Time Lord's new face. The action soon shifts to a toy factory in London where 'new management' has taken over and is working on new products. These include shop-window dummies and replicas of famous people (for use in place of waxworks). It's clear that something strange is going on and, once the Doctor recovers and begins working with UNIT, their attention focuses on the factory. The situation slowly escalates: the Brigadier's attempts to investigate are blocked by a superior, General Scobie (actually an Auton replica), while the Autons produced at the factory recover the missing sphere by killing Seeley. Eventually, a crisis is reached and in the final episode Autons break out of their shop-windows while the Doctor attempts to destroy the Nestene Consciousness which has been grown in a vat at the factory.

Names in *Doctor Who* often seem to be just collections of random syllables, but the Autons are an exception. The term works as a contraction of 'automatic' or 'automaton', and one of the central things about their appeal is their being a product of *repetition*, and so devoid of individual features. Autons have no agency or identity of their own save what they derive from their controlling consciousness. That identity may seem like a human (as with the replica of General Scobie, or later of Mickey in *Rose*) but will look plastic, unconvincing, fake. The first shots of the plastics factory (in Episode 2 of the story) are presumably documentary ones of real plastic dolls being made. The images are disturbing: moulds shaped like babies' heads ready to be dipped in plastic; a box full of identical pink heads; eyes being punched into the heads with unaltering mechanical force. So the Autons are scary not just because shop-window dummies can be found everywhere, but because they look human but aren't.

Allied to this is what might be called plastic phobia, a sense that things made of plastic are somehow unnatural. The Autons' second appearance, in *Terror of the Autons* (also by Holmes) makes much play with this. There is an animate plastic troll-doll, a plastic armchair that swallows up the person sitting in it, a telephone flex that strangles the Doctor and plastic daffodils that shoot out a transparent film to suffocate the person holding them. There are also Autons equipped with identical smiling carnival heads to distribute the daffodils. Indeed, *Terror of the Autons* can be understood best as a series of set pieces showing ways in which things made of plastic can be used to scare children.

It's clear that these sorts of qualities in the Autons fitted very well with the kind of series that Russell T Davies wanted to create when he and his team brought back *Doctor Who* in 2005. The revived series is more often based on contemporary Earth than it had been at almost any point since the Pertwee era; moreover, it often plays on everyday experiences and fears. Andrew Pixley's *The Doctor Who Companion: Season One* (2005) reprints the synopsis document for the 2005 season, which includes the following comments from Davies:

If the Zogs on planet Zog are having trouble with the Zog-monster…who gives a toss? But if a +human+ colony on the planet Zog is in trouble, a last outpost of humanity fighting to survive…then I'm interested.

Every story, somehow, should come back to Earth, to human-ity, its ancestors and its descendants. (42)

This concern to root the series in the everyday made the Autons a logical choice to be featured in *Rose*, the first episode of the revived series; it also gives an idea of the impetus behind Davies' most prominent innovation in their use. About half-way through the episode, Rose's boyfriend, Mickey, is waiting for her in an ordinary street. He hears a noise and goes to see what its source is. It seems to be coming from a wheelie bin. He opens it to look inside and find what the source is, but he finds his fingers are stuck to the lid. The bin growls and advances on him, eventually pulling him back cartoonishly into its maw and giving a satisfied burp. As Davies says in the DVD commentary to *Rose*, he found himself hoping that, for children who had watched the programme, the next week-day would be one where bins were put out on their street, so that they could imagine what could be inside or whether the bins might capture them.

Davies also returns to the idea, from the earlier Auton stor-ies, that plastic is somehow unnatural, and indeed adds to it with contemporary concerns about pollution. At one point in *Rose*, he gives the following exchange of dialogue:

ROSE: And, this living plastic…What's it got against us?

THE DOCTOR: Nothing. It loves you. You've got such a good planet, lots of smoke and oil, plenty of toxins and diox-ins in the air – just what the Nestene Consciousness needs. Its foodstock was destroyed in the War, all its protein planets rotted. So. Earth. Dinner. (Davies et al. 2005, 35)

This adds to the sense that the Autons are consistently shown as warnings against the excesses of mass-production con-sumerism. In *Spearhead from Space*, when they break out of the shop-windows, they are of course doing so while wearing the latest fashions, and with the price-tags visibly attached. The effect is even more pronounced when *Rose* replicates the same image. Thirty-five years of accumulated TV technique between the two mean that the earlier story's gritty realism is replaced by glossy perfection. Even when they are static in their windows, the Autons are beautifully lit and impeccably dressed. They are, in short, just what viewers might walk past and be enticed by on any normal shopping day. To see them break out and turn on their consumers in such spectacular fashion can't help but feel like a warning.

By Davies' account, the BBC took some convincing to use the Autons as the monsters in the first episode. As he said in a 2005 interview with Benjamin Cook:

> ... the BBC was worried – we had more conversations about the Autons than anything else. Until I wrote it, it looked like an old monster. But you can waste a lot of time trying to be original. It doesn't have to be original: it just has to be good. When I'd written the script, they saw what I'd meant, that actually the Autons are in the background. They're a plot device so that the Doctor and Rose can meet. (Cook, 2005a, 15)

That tends to downplay the importance of the Autons to *Rose*, especially in the light of this description in the same interview by Davies of the characteristics of his writing:

> 'Fast. Cheeky. Colourful. Good laughs. Proper drama. And specifically – this is the thing that enticed me to do Doctor Who – big pictures. Television doesn't do that enough; most television is people sitting there talking. I always try to write big pictures, and it drives people mad because the budget goes to hell.' (13)

If nothing else, what the Autons enable in *Rose* is its big pictures: the three or four most memorable images that define it. The episode doesn't have the scope to spend as much time as the earlier stories on the Autons, even if it wanted to, because of two main constraints: its relative brevity (45 minutes, compared to the earlier stories' four 25-minute episodes), and the multitude of other work it has to do, introduce the Doctor, Rose, the TARDIS, and send them off together. So Davies has to cherry-pick the bits of the mythos that seem most spectacular.

In *Terror of the Autons*, after the incident in which the Doctor has been rescued by the Brigadier from being strangled by his phone flex, 'Remember what I told you, Brigadier? The Nestenes can put life into anything made of plastic. Anything at all.' The Brigadier replies, in his most stoic and doom-laden voice, 'I see. And there's a lot of plastic around.' *Terror of the Autons* could be seen as an extended riff on this one line. As noted above, it takes a whole variety of mildly creepy things that could be made out of plastic and turns them into actively creepy, quasi-sentient things. In that sense, it could be regarded as the most opportunistic *Doctor Who* story ever. Plastic was, after all, not as universal in 1971 as it is now, and must have seemed newer and stranger then. Even now, in comparison to objects made of wood or metal, plastic things seem slightly artificial or fake.

In fact, *Terror of the Autons* compounds this sense by having a plot thread based around a travelling circus that's used to spread the Autons' deadly plastic daffodils. If plastic is a good subject for horror because of its 'fakeness' and opposition to 'natural' materials, so are circuses because they're places of *forced* jollity and happiness. (As witness, for instance, the range of stories – including in *Doctor Who* – about scary clowns.) So *Terror of the Autons* features a group of Autons with identical smiling carnival heads distributing their deadly flowers throughout the UK. The scariest thing about them, though, is not particularly the flowers; on some level, the viewer always knows that the Doctor will defeat any mass threat to humanity. The scariest thing is their identical, unchanging smiles, parading up and down the screen. Smiles are supposed to be spontaneous, human gestures. When they're something that can be manufactured and cloned, somehow they're scarier than no expression at all. The Autons are so effective as monsters because you know that thousands more could roll off the same endless production line.

A last Auton cameo in the 2010 season finale, *The Pandorica Opens/The Big Bang*, underlines this point. The plot of these stories is too complicated to summarise briefly; indeed, it is almost too complicated to understand, even after repeated viewing, but the basic premise is as follows: the Doctor and his companion, Amy Pond, find themselves in Roman Britain, where a legendary artefact known as the Pandorica has been buried under Stonehenge. The Pandorica, a kind of prison-box, has been designed to cage 'the most feared being in the universe', and over the course of the first episode appears to be opening. Meanwhile, the Doctor and Amy encounter a Roman centurion who appears to be Amy's fiancé Rory. Rory was apparently killed a few episodes earlier, and remembers nothing between his death and reappearance in this world. At the climax of *The Pandorica Opens*, two traps are sprung. Firstly, the Pandorica is revealed to be empty, but designed by an alliance of all the Doctor's enemies. It is designed to cage the Doctor himself, and he is forced into it. Secondly, Rory is revealed to be an Auton duplicate, and he shoots Amy. As the episode ends, there appears to be no hope left.

The Rory-Auton is by far the most convincing duplicate seen on the programme: he doesn't have the shiny skin of the Scobie duplicate in *Spearhead from Space* or the stuck-record speech patterns of the Mickey duplicate in *Rose*. His apparent authenticity makes his betrayal of Amy all the more powerful. But this is unashamedly the Autons being used as a plot device. Once Amy is dead, the duplicate starts to recover his humanity, and sets in motion the chain of actions that unpicks all the earlier disasters. The only property of the Autons needed for this plot is their fakeness: Rory could just as easily have been a generic robot like, say, those seen in *The Androids of Tara* (1978). But for those who know the Autons' past appearances, there's another layer of meaning here about the fakeness of plastic: nothing about it can be believed.

THE WEEPING ANGELS
(2007, 2010)

By some measures, Steven Moffat is the most popular author ever to have written for *Doctor Who*. He contributed one story to each of the four seasons broadcast from 2005 to 2008. Two of those, *The Empty Child/The Doctor Dances* (2005) and *Blink* (2007), have topped *Doctor Who Magazine*'s annual 'Season survey' of fans' opinions. Both of those episodes won the World Science Fiction Convention's Hugo Award, as did *The Girl in the Fireplace* (2006) and *The Pandorica Opens/The Big Bang* (2010). No other Doctor Who stories have ever won Hugos. The announcement of Moffat as successor to Russell T Davies in the role of 'showrunner' from 2010 was greeted with almost universal acclaim. Even the brief scene he wrote for the BBC's Children in Need telethon, *Time Crash* (2007), managed to mingle good jokes with a knotty time paradox in just eight minutes.

Moffat spoke about his fondness for the use of time travel as a *Doctor Who* plot element in an interview in *Doctor Who Magazine* (Bailey, 2008):

> Time travel is, I think, the magic element of *Doctor Who*...People witter on about going to other planets,

which *Doctor Who* has never really done, it's just gone to a forest – but the magic of Doctor Who is that he travels in *time*. Travelling in space is just engineering, but travelling in time is witchcraft.

There has been a tendency to regard his time travelling as just a delivery system...and I think that's absolutely right and proper 99% of the time, to be honest. I think if you carried on doing tricksy things with time, all the time, then it would get very tedious very fast. But now and then, I think it's a good thing to exploit that. What must it be like to be a man who presumably has no clue what age he is? Because the calendar means nothing to him and, unless he's counting the days on a wall, it's a complete blank to him. He must have continuing friendships with people that he also thinks of as long dead. He says things like 'I used to know Admiral Nelson.' But he should *currently* know him. He's probably got dinner booked with him! That, I think, is a fun idea – it's one that I think has to be rationed, but we could turn it up a bit. A bit more of that would be fun. Especially because children are quite excited by time travel – in a way, more so than going to other planets. Going to the past is actually impossible. Going to other planets is a matter of a long-enough railway track. (49)

Blink was the most elaborate working-out of the consequences of time travel that had been seen in *Doctor Who* up to that point, and the monsters it contains are designed with ruthless precision to drive the story and terrify children. In the DWM preview for *Blink* (Cook, 2007), Moffat says that he volunteered to do this episode – which because of schedule and budget constraints would have both a limited effects budget and only fleeting appearances by the Doctor – to make amends for having backed out of writing episodes scheduled for earlier in the same season. The result is a story whose structural experimentation mirrors what its monsters can do.

Blink begins as a haunted house story. A young woman named Sally Sparrow climbs a gate at night and enters an old, deserted mansion, seemingly to take photos of its state of decay. It is 2007. In one room, she finds peeling wallpaper which she pulls back to reveal a message addressed to her by name. It tells her to 'beware the weeping angels' and to duck. Just as she does so, a stone breaks through a window behind her. She turns her torch to see who threw it, but sees nothing except a statue of a weeping angel, its hands covering its face.

To summarise the full plot of *Blink* would take many hundreds of words. But, in brief, the statue is a member of an alien race called the Weeping Angels. Four of them are stranded on Earth around this house; their goal is to capture the Doctor's TARDIS. The Doctor himself is stranded in the 1960s without his time machine. Through the course of the story, Sally must discover a way to rescue him and remove the threat of the Angels.

The Angels are a race of alien predators with two extra-ordinary characteristics. First, they gain their energy from sending their victims back in time. Second, they are 'quantum-locked': that is, they can only move when they are not being observed. (And when they move, they move fast.) So when a character near them blinks, it allows them to reach out and touch him. *Blink*'s intricacy is entirely bound up with the nature of the monsters it depicts. On one level, the Weeping Angels are clearly aimed at scaring children. A montage of shots of similar statues at the end of the episode is surely meant to suggest that quantum-locked time-hungry Weeping Angels could be found in any town. Though Moffat provides a kind of rationale for their being unable to move while observed – the Doctor says it's an adaptive defence mechanism – it's far easier to understand in terms of, say, the playground game of Grandmother's Footsteps.

But the Doctor's talk of defence mechanisms is at least a useful pointer to one idea about the Weeping Angels: they are niche creatures, in the sense described in the Introduction. They have a fairly limited range of ways by which they can attack humans and, by the same token, a fairly limited range of potential stories in which they can appear. Moffat's monsters have tended so far to be in this category. They are the manifestation of some single evolutionary drive or need, pursued ruthlessly to the exclusion of all others. They tend, therefore, not to have much in the way of personality or even voice. (Of the four monsters created by Moffat up until 2008, only one says anything substantive, the Vashta Nerada from *Silence in the Library/Forest of the Dead* (2008), and they use someone else's voice.) The role of the Doctor or, in *Blink*, Sally, is to understand what that evolutionary necessity is and find a way to use it against the Angels and so neutralise them.

In the case of *Blink*, one can press the argument further. The Weeping Angels are defeated by their nature, by their strength. The final image of them, locked in their circle around the TARDIS, is one of the neatest and most symmetrical ones ever found in the series. (On the DVD commentary for *Blink*, Moffat says that he happened upon this ending almost by accident; he had placed four Angels in the house, and only after much head scratching about how to defeat them did he realise how this worked with the four sides of the TARDIS police box.) So just as the Weeping Angels' method of attack is one that would work for no other creature, so is the method by which they're defeated.

Throughout *Blink*, Sally – a human who's otherwise had no contact with the Doctor's world – is depicted as *learning*, figuring out, adapting. It's clear that she's very good at this, and certainly better than some of the other humans around her. It may be, of course, that the Weeping Angels learn too, but they certainly don't find any way to break out of their evolutionary niche. And even if Sally's adaptability isn't quite what defeats the Angels, it certainly gets her much further into discovering the Angels' nature than anyone else had up to that point. That's a consistent theme of *Doctor Who:* that rationality and scientific enquiry will always be able to provide explanations for any happening, no matter how bizarre. Magic (as I'll discuss in the chapter on the Dæmons) is always just a word used to cover scientific phenomena that can't yet be explained. Sally's first action in *Blink* is the very Doctorish one of letting her curiosity take her somewhere she's not supposed to go, the Angels' house. So it's not just, as I suggested in the Introduction, that monsters have a narrow outlook and humans (potentially at least) a broad one. Humans can change, and monsters rarely can. In the case of the Autons, which are puppeted by their controlling consciousness, there is presumably no scope for free will at all. The Weeping Angels may be able to escape their nature, but aren't shown doing so. This fixity in monsters' nature makes them more implacable but also more predictable, and it is an idea that I'll return to in future chapters.

The Weeping Angels returned in *The Time of Angels/Flesh and Stone* (2010), a very different kind of story, *Aliens* to Blink's *Alien*. It's set in the future, where a spaceship carrying an Angel in its hold has crash-landed on a planet containing more of them. This is a story with the Doctor at its centre, very much shaped around big spectacle. It entirely dispenses with the Angels' power to send people back in time, and instead depicts them physically attacking people, for instance, by breaking their necks. It does, however, augment their abilities with a new one. Early in the story, the Doctor finds a book about the creatures saying that 'The image of an Angel is itself an Angel'. That is, if an image of an Angel is looked at for long enough, for instance, on a screen, it will emerge from the screen and itself become real. This does in fact happen to the Doctor's companion, Amy, in a sequence that shows Moffat's dedication to scaring children at its peak. Because if an Angel can step out of a screen at Amy, why can't it step out of the television screen on which children are watching *Doctor Who*?

This is a peculiar characteristic of some of Moffat's monsters: they're designed, as it were, to be interactive, to reach out beyond the TV show and have children thinking about them in real life. As with the montage at the end of Blink, or the Vashta Nerada of *Silence in the Library* inhabiting any shadow, these are concepts that are *applicable*, that can be transferred to a child's everyday life. The further Moffat goes down this route, admittedly, the more visible it is that this is what he's doing. And at some point, surely, he will run out of childhood fears to appropriate. But at his best, he's as ruthless as Robert Holmes in *Terror of the Autons* in his search for ways to insinuate ideas from *Doctor Who* into everyday life.

KROLL (1979)

One of *Doctor Who*'s earliest experiments in structure was the *Key to Time* season (1978–79). Each of the season's six stories was framed as the Doctor's quest for one of the six segments of the Key to Time, an awesomely powerful, indeed, almost mystical object needed to restore balance to the universe. Each of the six segments (fragments of a crystal cube) was originally disguised as something else. The Doctor and his companion, Romana, are equipped with a 'tracer', a device that enables them to locate the segment and then convert it into its true form as a segment of the Key.

In most of the six stories, the segment's disguised form is something valuable but with no special properties. However, the fifth story, *The Power of Kroll* (1979), does something rather more unusual with the idea of this kind of hidden power. Like the first two Auton stories, it was written by Robert Holmes. Indeed, it was his last story for the series before a number of years away from it and then a triumphant return with *The Caves of Androzani* (1984), Peter Davison's last appearance as the Doctor and, by common consent, one of the series' all-time classics. *The Power of Kroll* is generally reckoned something of a disappointment, though its most obvious flaws are those of production rather than script. I want, among other things, to argue that the script is one of the series' most interesting and adventurous, not least in the way it deals with its monster.

According to Miles and Wood (2004b, 250), the story emerged from a brief given to Holmes of creating the biggest monster the series had seen. Holmes' chosen setting was a marshy world, a 'moon of Delta Magna'. He creates an intriguingly complex situation by setting out four different parties for the Doctor and Romana to encounter. The first is the indigenous population of the moon, a green-skinned race known as the 'Swampies'. The second is the crew of a drilling rig from the moon's home planet of Delta Magna: they extract gas from the swamp in order to fuel Delta Magna's industries. The third is a gun runner, Rohm-Dutt, covertly supplying the Swampies with weapons to enable them to resist the offworld occupation of their moon. And the fourth is Kroll itself, a giant octopoid monster that occasionally rises from the waters. Kroll has been disturbed by the activities of the drilling rig and is about to become active again after a period of quiescence; the Swampies also worship it.

In a sense, Kroll is 'pure' monster, a force of nature like the Weeping Angels that destroys, feeds and is ultimately defeated by the hero. It does not speak or communicate; it only fulfils its needs. The fact that it is worshipped by the Swampies is an interesting complication, though hardly unique. There is a very similar situation in the movie *King Kong* (1933) and its many successors and remakes. Holmes does, however, bring a series of complications to this basic set up. None of the parties I described in the previous paragraph is free of moral ambiguity. The Swampies are hostile, defensive and threaten the Doctor and Romana with death on several occasions. The crew of the drilling rig are exploiting the environment of the moon without comprehending the implications of what they're doing, and they are wilfully blind to many of the consequences of their actions. Rohm-Dutt, as a gun runner, is a morally complex figure from the start, all the more so because he's not bringing the Swampies their weapons out of the goodness of his heart or belief in their cause. He is in fact being paid by Thawn, the commander on the drilling rig, to give them faulty weapons that will both sabotage their resistance efforts and discredit the environmental 'Sons of Earth' movement supporting them. And Kroll, to coin a phrase, is beyond good and evil, hardly to be blamed for following its hungers, but needing to be fought and resisted too. It has to be said that, to contemporary eyes, the story gets partway towards being an intriguing parable of colonial exploitation but it is sabotaged by its patronising treatment of the Swampies. They are depicted as primitive, superstitious, hidebound by their traditions and just as greedy for power in their own way as those running the drilling rig.

Most of the action of *The Power of Kroll* follows the Doctor and Romana bouncing back and forth between these various parties until the Doctor has finally figured out enough about the true situation to take the action he needs to defeat Kroll. The swamp is full of tiny octopoid creatures, like Kroll but only a few inches across. The Doctor's logic (though only explained in retrospect) is that one of these must have ingested the fifth segment of the Key to Time and, mutated by its power, grown to Kroll's size. So what he does, at a point of, seemingly, terminal disaster on the drilling rig, is to venture out onto one of its platforms with the tracer to detect segments of the Key. He's almost immediately attacked by Kroll, but manages to jam the tracer into the monster's body. There's a blinding flash, the monster is gone, and the Doctor has the crystalline fifth segment of the Key on the end of the tracer. Almost incidentally, the drilling rig's operations have been crippled, and the disturbance they caused to the moon's environment seem unlikely to resume. The Swampies and the people of Delta Magna don't exactly have a future of unbridled peace and co-operation ahead of them, but there is at least the chance for more mutual understanding.

The strange thing about *The Power of Kroll* is that without the presence of the monster, it's a story that could be transferred to any number of venues in our own time in which the developed world exploits the developing world. As I said before, the treatment of the native people would

doubtless need to be more nuanced, but otherwise the political dynamic is one around which many stories could be built.
So what is the monster there for? What does this science-
fictional element bring to the story? Well, the presence of a
mile-wide, incessantly hungry, unpredictable octopus always
adds a certain amount of jeopardy. And it gives the Doctor
a clear adversary, something to structure the story around in
an otherwise grey moral landscape. (It has to be said that the
execution of Kroll is one of the weakest aspects of the production. Even on the restored DVD version, which fixes some
of the most egregious blunders, it's still very visibly a small
model creature composited into location footage, or men-
acing an equally small model of the rig.) Kroll is, as it were, a
pure monster, pure threat. Like the Autons and the Weeping
Angels, there's no suggestion that it could be anything other
than that. If Kroll had worked as a spectacle, and it might
be a tall order, even in today's era of computer-generated
imagery, *The Power of Kroll* might be far better remembered
both as a 'romp' and a story with more serious undertones.
But not for the first or the last time, it's one of the occasions when *Doctor Who's* ambition exceeded what could be
realised.

THE PRIMORDS (1970)

Jon Pertwee's first season as the Doctor, which began with his encounter with the Autons in *Spearhead from Space*, ended with *Inferno* (1970). Between these were two seven-part stories with notably complex storylines, *Doctor Who and the Silurians* (1970) and *The Ambassadors of Death* (1970): see Chapters 11 and 26, respectively. By the time they reached the end of the season, audiences might well have got the message that life in the Pertwee era was not going to be as simple as in previous versions of *Doctor Who*. Admittedly, there was then some retreat from this; Pertwee's second season, and subsequent ones, were a little more traditional and predictable. But *Inferno* in particular is the zenith of a specific approach to the series.

All of its seven episodes take place on a scientific research and drilling base somewhere in England. The team there is engaged in trying to drill through the Earth's crust to release the pockets of 'Stahlman's gas' beneath it, a potential source of energy that will render other fuel sources obsolete. Right from the start, though, it's clear that the project has problems. An engineer sent to repair a drillhead problem discovers a strange greenish slime bubbling up through one of the output pipes. He touches the slime – it's blazingly hot – and stumbles out into the open air in a kind of stupor. He is soon transformed into a hairy, grunting monster. He assaults other workers seemingly without reason, and loses any kind of rationality. When the Doctor and UNIT's chief, Brigadier Lethbridge-Stewart, find him and are forced to kill him, the patch of wall against which his body falls is scorched black. But this strange incident does not deter the leader of the project, Professor Stahlman, who seems obsessive in his desire to carry it through. Various figures around him attempt to slow drilling so that the penetration of the Earth's crust will be as safe as possible, but Stahlman disregards their advice.

The Doctor has acceded to the Brigadier's request to investigate the project because of an ulterior motive. He is using the project's nuclear power plant to fuel his experiments to get the TARDIS working again. About a third of the way through the story, one of these experiments works, after a fashion. The TARDIS console propels him through to the same place in a parallel world. In this world, the UK is a fascist republic. The drilling project is still taking place, but it is more advanced. Each of the people in the Doctor's 'own' world has an equivalent in the parallel one, but they are far more subordinated to the ruthless needs of their regime. As their project approaches the point of penetration of the Earth's crust, an unbearable noise is heard. The Doctor says it is the sound of the planet 'screaming out its rage'. In this other world, there are also far more of the feral creatures on the prowl. (The credits refer to them as 'Primords', but they are not named as such onscreen.) They are difficult to kill, being resistant to gunshots, and seem only to be properly deterred by the threat of extreme cold. They can also transmit the 'infection' of the slime by touch, which is, of course, unbearably hot. They make a high-pitched screeching sound, which (according to the Doctor) is the same as that heard at Krakatoa in 1883.

Ultimately, the drilling project in the fascist world succeeds. The Earth's crust is penetrated, and it soon becomes clear that the energies released are too great to be contained. Volcanic eruptions are occurring everywhere, and the temperature is rising apocalyptically. Uniquely in *Doctor Who*, we are shown the beginning of the end of the world. With no way out, the Doctor is powerless to intervene. As he departs the parallel world at the end of the sixth episode, the remaining characters are left behind to face certain death along with that of the Earth. The last episode's action, in which this disaster is averted in 'our' world, is a relative anticlimax.

The overall pattern of *Inferno* is a familiar one for the science fiction field. The clear message is that there are things that humanity is not meant to meddle with, and if they do, the consequences will be dire. This is a story at least as old as that of Faust, who sold his soul for knowledge. But unlike Faust in the various tellings of the story, Stahlman seems not to have any insight into his condition, or into the consequences of his actions. At the one point when he might, after the penetration of the crust in the alternate world, he is rapidly becoming transformed into a Primord. (In both worlds, he conceals an infection from the green slime for a long period before finally descending into the monstrous state.)

The Primords themselves are as the name suggests: primordial, primitive. They lack the power of speech, and though they seem to have some basic intelligence (they hunt in packs, for instance), they lack much of what distinguishes humans from animals. What's most distinctive about them is their strength, their association with heat and the sense that their kind of primitive existence is *contagious*. They do not seem to kill from any motive; they assault people who are not threats to them and do not, for instance, feed off the corpses. (Although that would probably be too disturbing an idea to be shown in *Doctor Who*.) They are, simply, violent and destructive. Humanity has descended into the same state as Kroll.

As my paraphrase of the story of *Inferno* suggests, the Primords are not the Doctor's main antagonist in the story. They are one plot device among several, and appear at various points throughout the narrative to provide jeopardy for the Doctor and increase the tension. So there's a sense in which the Primords are not essential to the story, and one could imagine it without them. What they add to the story, though, is a kind of fantastical heightening. If the drilling simply caused earthquakes or eruptions, it might be understandable as causing the sort of disaster that takes place in the real world. The presence of the Primords makes it clear that the stakes in *Inferno* are higher. They also serve as a contrast to the choices the humans make in both worlds. Around Stahlman is a small staff, along with the forces of UNIT, who have the chance to avert (or not) the oncoming disaster. Almost as soon as the Doctor returns to his 'own' world, having seen the imminent destruction of the fascist alternative, he's led to muse 'So...free will is not an illusion.' However relentless the drilling process may seem, there is always the choice available to stop it. The Primords are depicted as being less than human because they lack the faculty to choose and to reason. It might also be suggested that the fascist state is shown as being closer to Primord-nature than the Doctor's own world in two ways. First, as noted before, there are far more Primords in the fascist-republic-world. Second, the attributes of the fascist state, brutality, violence, lack of individuality, are very much closer to the attributes of the Primords than those of the Doctor's world. So the fascist world is a step away from ours and toward the primitivism that the Primords represent.

It's worth saying that, at the time when *Inferno* was broadcast, the UK was in the early stages of exploring and exploiting the oil reserves in the North Sea. Though it's difficult to read *Inferno* as a dire warning against the dangers of that process, it's obvious that some of the story's imagery comes from oil drilling. Indeed, one of the most sympathetic characters in both worlds is Keith Sutton, an oil drilling expert seconded to the Stalhman project. I think it's far more worth considering the implications of the title. The story was apparently called 'The Mo-Hole Project' (or variants on that) by its author, Don Houghton, until quite late in the production process. But 'Inferno', apart from being obviously a better title, also carries associations of Dante's great medieval poem *The Divine Comedy*. In the first of its three books, often called the *Inferno*, Dante journeys through hell (as conceived by the Catholic Church). He sees sinners punished, in progressively severe ways, as he descends through the circles of hell. Moreover, the sinners' punishments are often shaped to be appropriate to their crimes. So the lustful, for instance, are buffeted about by a perpetual storm.

The image of hell is summoned up explicitly in the first episode of the story, when Sutton hears that the drill is 20 miles down: 'You're liable to wake up old Nick going that deep!' he says, and he's told that this is why some technicians have nicknamed the project the Inferno. The story isn't, of course, about literally waking the devil. But it is, in some sense, a representative of a familiar category of *Doctor Who* stories: the possession story. Initially, you might say, the only person with the contagion is Stahlman, with his monomaniacal desire to complete the drilling regardless of the consequences or dangers. (He's repeatedly shown to be ignoring safety procedures to complete the drilling as soon as possible.) In the fascist state, with far less questioning of his will, the contagion is wider. As I suggested earlier, the Primords are a kind of literalised version of this contagion. The nature of the slime that causes the transformation into Primords is never explained, but it makes sense in the terms the story has set up, as an early symptom of the apocalypse to come.

Towards the end of the story in the fascist-republic thread of *Inferno*, there are some surreal scenes set outside on the base. Filmed in such a way as to suggest the burning heat that's now inescapable, they show the Primords moving around in a world almost devoid of 'true' human life. This, the story seems to be saying, is the logical endpoint, both of Stahlman's overweening ambition and the authoritarian world that has fed it. And the Primords are a warning: If this goes on, humans will end up in their animal state. This is hell, and nor are they out of it.

THE BORAD (1985)

*T*imelash (1985) is widely regarded as one of the worst serials ever broadcast as part of *Doctor Who*, amid, one has to say, some stern competition. It has a weak script, cheap-looking design, unimaginative direction, laughable special effects and some appalling performances. But it's not all bad. The central villain, the Borad, is depicted by Robert Ashby in a way that elevates his menace to an entirely different level from the rest of the story. It's unfortunate, therefore, that the story takes so long to get to him.

Timelash is set almost entirely on the planet Karfel, where a cowed population live under the rule of a kindly old man named the Borad. Only ever appearing to the people via television screens, he seems to be devoted to research that will benefit his people. There is, however, a rebel movement on Karfel, who operate in fear of being subject to the Borad's ultimate punishment, which is being thrown into a device called the Timelash. This is in effect a portal that takes the victim back to another point in time and space; as the story starts, it points to Scotland in the Middle Ages. The Doctor arrives on the planet with his companion, Peri, and they soon meet both the official leadership of Karfel, the Borad's representative in the outer world, known as the Maylin, and the rebels. The Borad's leadership is also about to provoke another confrontation, a war with a species from a neighbouring planet, the Bandrils. Rather unusually, it's also stated that the Doctor made a visit to the planet before in an untelevised adventure during his third incarnation.

At this point, the story diverges into two strands. The Doctor is forced by the Maylin to go back down the Timelash's path to retrieve the last person who had passed down it. She has an amulet that the Borad needs. Meanwhile, Peri is held hostage in a cave beneath the city to ensure the Doctor's co-operation; while there, she is threatened by the 'Morlox', savage lizard-like creatures. The Doctor's path down the time corridor takes him to the banks of a Scottish lake, not in the Middle Ages as originally predicted, but in 1885. There he retrieves not only the Timelash victim he was sent for, but also a young man named Herbert. All three return to Karfel. Meanwhile, Peri's plight continues, as is often the case for Doctor Who companions. Not only is she being threatened by the Morlox, she is also about to suffer the effects of a gas that will merge her human form with that of the Morlox. The Borad's motive is soon exposed when the Doctor returns and encounters him in person. The kindly old man who appears on the screens is just an android, at the service of the real Borad. He was originally a scientist named Megelen, whom the Doctor encountered on his previous visit. Megelen had been conducting experiments on the Morlox; he is now a half-human, half-Morlox hybrid who considers himself disgusting in appearance.

So the Borad, like Stahlman in *Inferno*, is another depiction of the scientist as Faustian overreacher. The difference between the two is that, in the case of Stahlman, the corruption caused by his work is a visible, generalised contagion: the green slime and the transformation it brings into the Primord form. In *Timelash*, only the Borad himself is a human-transformed-into-monstrosity. So far as there's a contagion in the story, it's in the state of the society as a whole. Though it's crudely depicted and on a tiny scale, the politics of Karfel are clearly corrupt. As in *Vengeance on Varos*, a story broadcast earlier in the same season, the world of *Timelash* is clearly an oppressive surveillance state. The rebel movement is one symptom of this. So too is Karfel's arbitrary and capricious justice system and its overbearing paternalism (seemingly more benign than, but actually very similar to, the fascist state in *Inferno*).

There is, however, one crucial difference between the Borad and Stahlman-as-Primord: the Borad can speak. This, it seems to me, is one of the most crucial distinctions one can make about monsters. A creature like Kroll is pure appetite. The Borad's case is different. Not only can he speak, he's actually hugely intelligent. So he can be asked to show mercy, and he can refuse. The implication is that his monstrous behaviour is a choice, something he could escape if the Doctor helped him to redeem himself. But *Timelash* is not that kind of story.

From the point when the Doctor encounters the Borad, the story resolves itself in fairly predictable ways. The Doctor defeats the Borad, twice, in fact, since Megelen had made a clone of himself. The attack from the Bandrils, provoked by the Borad, is averted, and peace seems to be in the offing. 'Herbert', whom the Doctor brought from Scotland, turns out to be the young H G Wells, and he ends up taking the inspiration for his science fiction novels from what he has seen on Karfel.

What's most notable about the story, as suggested earlier, is the way that Ashby's performance renders the Borad a far more interesting villain than most encountered in the series. Given lines like 'And you have betrayed me' or 'I would guard your tongue, Time Lord', he very deliberately underplays them, rather than making the character the usual fortissimo lunatic. The performance is augmented by some superb prosthetics showing his half-Morlox nature. As a result, the production does actually create the emotional effect that most such stories make only a token gesture towards: that the Borad is a creature who needs to be pitied as well as defeated.

The depiction of the Borad does, however, bring up a rather more troubling issue with monsters in general. Monsters are monstrous both in appearance and in their moral state. (For this reason, I only consider in this book creatures that do actually look monstrous.) With the Borad, there's an explicit causal link between the two. Moral deformity is seen to entail physical deformity, so that physical deformity itself comes to be seen as a marker of evil. That's a rather worrying way of seeing things, especially since in the real world many people suffer deformities of greater or lesser seriousness through no fault of their own. (A similar point is made about *Timelash* by Miles and Wood, 2005, p. 147, although they address the question of whether *Doctor Who*, and similar shows, tend to *exploit* mutilation.)

There is, of course, a long tradition of monsters whose moral and physical deformity reflect on each other. The various tellings of *The Phantom of the Opera* are the obvious example, and the Borad can be seen as sitting in that tradition, particularly given his desire to possess beauty in the form of Peri. The previous season's story, *The Caves of Androzani*, featured a very similar figure, Sharaz Jek, though his scarring was due to another's treachery rather than to his own actions. And in fact, the Borad and Jek belong with Stahlman in a subset of the Phantom tradition: scientists whose Faustian overreaching is punished. The most famous example of this is probably Davros (see Chapter 16).

More generally, villains in comics are often defined by their scarring. In the Batman mythos, for instance, the Joker acquires his villainous identity through falling in a vat of chemicals that leave his face with the colours of a clown. A similar origin of story defines Two-Face, who literally has a 'good' (that is, unmarked) side of his face and an 'evil', scarred one.

I'm sure *Doctor Who* occasionally makes stories in which expectations generated by appearances are subverted. The most obvious example is *Galaxy 4+* (1965), featuring a race of beautiful female Drahvins and ugly, boar-like Rills. Only after some wrong turns do the Doctor and his companions deduce that the Drahvins are the power that needs to be fought, and the Rills protected. Far more frequent is the picture in which monsters that look uglier than humanity are also morally less worthy. Of the creatures considered in this book, that would certainly include the Sontarans, the Sycorax and the Toclafane. *The Claws of Axos* (see next chapter) also makes deliberate play with this concept, without ever quite escaping it.

So, to return to the original point, the Borad (as played by Ashby) is an interesting performance because he plays his lines not only against the stereotype of the *Doctor Who* villain, but also against the idea of monstrousness. In a character such as the Borad, the monstrousness is literally made external, in the shape of his physical deformity. And if a character's appearance is so overtly monstrous, why not his speech too? Ashby's voice, though, is untreated, mostly quiet and calm. He is almost always in control of himself and the situation, a reminder that he was, and still is, a scientist and a detached observer. His plans may be abhorrent, but his tone is often no more severe than that of a bank manager calling in an overdue loan. If the Borad could be separated out from the story that surrounds him, and sadly he can't, he would surely be remembered as one of the most interesting monsters to grace the series.

THE AXONS (1971)

In discussing *Timelash*, I talked a lot about beauty and ugliness. *The Claws of Axos* (1971) also plays with these ideas. It's another case in which a potentially interesting script is let down by a less than stellar production. Indeed, of all the stories from Jon Pertwee's time as the Doctor, it's the one I find hardest to watch without wincing, at the quality of the acting, at the limitations of the production and at the dated and distracting music. But it's worth persevering to try to understand what's at the root of the story.

Made only a year after *Inferno*, it takes off from the same topical problem, worries about a global energy shortage. The story begins with the arrival on Earth of a spaceship which buries itself in the ground near to the Nuton atomic power plant. The inhabitants of the ship soon reveal themselves. They call themselves Axons, and they are beautiful golden humanoids. They say that they need refuge on Earth. In return, they will give humanity the gift of axonite, a golden substance that can solve its energy needs. Axonite is a 'chameleon' substance; it can, for instance, cause animals to grow to much more than their usual size, with amazing consequences for the global food shortage. The Axons wish Axonite to be distributed across the globe.

Even before the story makes the point explicit, it's fairly clear to viewers that the Axons' story is a lie and a trap. The story's title is a broad hint in this direction, as are glimpses of the Axons' real form, grotesque orange-red tentacled monsters. The Axon spaceship captures anyone who comes near, including the Doctor. Once inside, he discovers that the Master is also held there, having been snared by the Axons in space. The spaceship, the Axons and Axonite, are in fact all one substance. Once it is spread across the world, the Axons will be able to suck the planet dry. The presence of a greedy, stupid government official named Chinn, who accepts the promise of Axonite unquestioningly, is also a clear pointer as to its real nature.

The trap was made even more clear by the story's original title, 'The Vampire from Space'. This is not an uncommon trope in written science fiction, probably its most famous telling is in Robert Sheckley's classic story 'The Leech' (1952). But the Axons differ from Dracula, at least, in presenting their offer in an initially tempting way. Axonite is, quite literally, too good to be true. Axonite is depicted as a snare because it's not *earned* – not something that humanity has worked to create for itself.

The Doctor's response to the offer of Axonite is interesting and, I think, meant to be instructive. In the scene in the first episode where the offer of Axonite is made to the humans, he asks a number of pointed questions about its nature. At that point, he's clearly undecided one way or another about whether the offer is genuine. He also stresses that Axonite will only bring material advantages: 'I doubt if even Axonite could increase the growth of human common sense.' What he does, therefore, is to *investigate*. The Doctor is always positioned, in theory, as a scientist, but his commitment to empiricism is only sometimes made concrete.

The Axonite is taken to the laboratory at the neighbouring nuclear power station. The Doctor takes a sample and places it in a cyclotron, with the intention of accelerating its particles to the speed of light, and so being able to unpack its structure: 'The idea is to split off a stream of Axonite particles and accelerate them through time. This way, we shall force it to analyse itself on the printout.' The idea is scientific nonsense, but it's beguiling nonsense. In the context of Axonite being an 'intelligent' substance, and the cyclotron being able to accelerate particles to the verge of light speed, it almost has a kind of coherence. In any case, the experiment goes disastrously wrong. As the cyclotron passes the speed of light, the Axons are told by their ship that their 'nutrition cycle' has been activated prematurely. They have to go to recover the Axonite. The Doctor sees that the Axonite is 'taking the whole output of Reactor One, absorbing it... and using it to grow.' In response, the laboratory is soon invaded by Axons in their natural form, the tentacled creatures seen earlier. They capture the Doctor and Jo and take them to Axos, their spaceship. But one important revelation comes out of this, that Axos, Axonite and the creatures who inhabit it (whether humanoid or not) are all one substance.

In the Doctor's absence, greed and short-sightedness run riot. Chinn, a government official depicted as almost comically blind to the dangers of Axos, begins the distribution of Axonite to all quarters of the world. The Master, having escaped from Axos, breaks into the Doctor's TARDIS. Meanwhile, the Axons try to extract from the Doctor the secrets of time travel. If they are able to venture anywhere in time and space, their feeding range will be hugely increased. Even within the conventions of *Doctor Who* – where real-world constraints are often glossed over in the interests of the story – the spread of Axonite happens with a kind of dreamlike speed. (Or, from the perspective of someone like the Doctor who realises its true nature, nightmarish speed.) Chinn and his colleagues seem to have accepted it so quickly as a panacea to the world's ills that there's no way for it to be stopped. In the story's terms, this is precisely because they haven't taken the step the Doctor did, of empiricism.

In fact, the analogy that springs to mind for Axonite is something like the philosopher's stone, the mythical substance sought by alchemists, which they thought would transform 'base metals' into gold. The golden skin of the Axons, and the colour of the Axonite, is surely not an accident. Gold has been seen as valuable in every culture and time, and the Axons' offer is meant to be tempting. But, as in stories like *Inferno*, miracle cures to the world's energy problems are too good to be true. The difference between *Inferno* and *The Claws of Axos* is that in the former story, the consequences of overreaching are depicted as a contagion of humans. Here, they're externalised, turned into a temptation that needs to be resisted. If he'd appeared in *Inferno*, Chinn would surely have been turned into a Primord and so doomed. Here, he's shown up as a blundering buffoon, but that's hardly the same.

The resolution of the story isn't really as interesting as its premise. The Doctor and the Master recognise the danger from Axos and, for once, forget their differences and cooperate. They conspire to use the Doctor's TARDIS to trap Axos in a 'time loop'. This does at least allow for some delightful rivalry-in-a-confined-space acting from Pertwee and Roger Delgado as the Master. And it is a reasonably fitting end, given the Axons' vampire nature; parasitic creatures are ultimately left with nothing but themselves to feed on. The main image the story leaves, though, is of the gap between what the Axons promise and what they really are. They and their gift may seem to be made of gold, but it's fool's gold.

THE DALEKS I (1963–64)

For the contemporary viewer, watching older *Doctor Who*, especially stories made in the black and white era before 1970, requires some allowances to be made. The pace is slower than contemporary television, of course, and the degree of visual sophistication is far less. In particular, the wealth of possibilities opened up by computer-generated imagery are not yet available. So, for instance, there are few techniques for showing large numbers of creatures or vast vistas. One has to accept that the world depicted will be overwhelmingly inhabited (and certainly run) by white males. And, inevitably, some scientific or historical ideas that might have seemed radical then will look outdated now. Watching *The Daleks* (1963–64), the series' second story, all of these provisos apply plus a few more. The story is very obviously studio-bound, and limitations of space and time clearly influenced its production. *Doctor Who* was still attempting to establish a tone, and one can see it evolving over the course of the story's seven episodes. The Daleks in this story are very different, and much weaker, than in their later appearances.

On the other hand, the earliest episodes have something remarkable that can only be dimly perceived now:

strangeness. Nowadays, we're so familiar with the premise of *Doctor Who* and the devices of science fiction that one of the series' dangers is that its marvels are too much *normalised*; this is a spacecraft, that's a cyborg, over there is a villain with powers X, Y and Z. Early *Doctor Who* is resolutely not normalised, because the series is still discovering what's possible. In addition, some techniques are brought to bear on it that are clearly new. Visual effects are one category here, in particular the weirdly abstract 'howlaround' title sequence that the series had in its early years. Sound and music are another. Ron Grainer's theme tune for the series has persisted up to the present day, and Delia Derbyshire's arrangement of it, as used in 1963, has been widely praised. Indeed, Derbyshire is now recognised as a pioneer of electronic music. The theme sounds, simply, as if it's not played on any recognisable instruments. There are elements that do orthodox things, a bassline, for instance, and a higher line carrying the melody. But it's impossible to tell how these sounds could be achieved. There's also an allied area of 'special sound', the sonic environments created for alien world. The obvious example to cite is the noise for the Dalek control room, a regular low pulsing that somehow manages to convey menace. With an admirable sense of its own history, the series has reused this effect right up to the Daleks' reappearance in *Victory of the Daleks* (2011).

The first Doctor Who story, *An Unearthly Child* (1963), begins in a contemporary London comprehensive school. Two teachers, Ian Chesterton and Barbara Wright. Puzzled by the curious behaviour of one of their students, Susan Foreman, they follow her to the address she has given as home and find that it is a junkyard. There they stumble upon the old man who claims to be her grandfather, the Doctor. Ian and Barbara stumble into the junkyard police-box that the Doctor seems weirdly protective of, and find to their astonishment that it is bigger on the inside than outside. Susan says it is called the TARDIS and it is their home. The Doctor is alarmed that he and Susan have been discovered; they are, he says, aliens, 'wanderers in the fourth dimension'. He activates the TARDIS and takes Ian, Barbara and Susan to another location, prehistoric Earth. There they encounter a group of cavepeople on the brink of discovering fire. The TARDIS crew barely escape with their lives, and the ship takes them to a new destination, a strange jungle. As they leave the safety of the TARDIS to explore, its radiation meter begins to rise to the danger zone.

The Daleks begins immediately after this cliffhanger. The forest in which the TARDIS has landed is petrified, seemingly after some great blast of heat. The Doctor's curiosity is piqued by this, even more so when the travellers see a huge city from a ledge in the forest. No inhabitants are visible, but it does at least seem to be intact despite whatever happened to the forest. The Doctor wants to explore, while Barbara wants to return to the TARDIS; so, in a piece of subterfuge typical of his character in this era, the Doctor empties the TARDIS' 'fluid links' of the mercury they need to function, and tells the others that they will have to visit the city to see if they can get some new supplies. Meanwhile, the others have begun to suspect that they are not alone in the forest, and the increased radiation is beginning to take its toll on them in the form of fatigue. Once the four travellers arrive at the city, they are immediately struck by its strange architecture: metal floors, low arches and a kind of antiseptic impersonality. They do not encounter any of its inhabitants until the end of the first episode. Barbara is separated from the others, and the last shots of the episode show her stepping back in horror from something moving towards her; all we are shown of this creature is a metal arm with a black plunger on its end.

This is, as we now know, a Dalek. Famously, a relatively brief description in Terry Nation's script was turned into an unforgettable design by the BBC's Raymond Cusick. Subsequently, *Doctor Who*'s designers often struggled to create monsters that broke up the human form and did not simply look like a man in a costume, but with the Daleks they succeeded at the first attempt. Whether the inspiration for their form came from a pepperpot or the Georgian State Dancers, accounts vary; they are unforgettably nonhuman. Their grating, mechanical voices only add to the effect. (Alwyn Turner's excellent 2011 biography of Terry Nation provides much valuable information both on the story itself and Nation's scriptwriting background beforehand. In particular, he makes it clear that Nation's previous experience adapting stories for the BBC series *Out of the Unknown* had immersed him in the magazine science fiction of the era.)

Early in the second episode, the Doctor and his other companions also are captured by the Daleks, and the back story slowly becomes clearer. At some point, a neutron bomb was detonated on this planet, irradiating all the living beings but leaving the buildings intact. The other side of this story is the Thals, the Daleks' opponents in the war that precipitated the bomb's detonation. They are now living in the jungle where the TARDIS landed, and they assist the travellers in various ways, for instance, by providing them with antiradiation drugs. However, the Thals are pacifists, reluctant to confront the Daleks.

For viewers who know the Daleks from their subsequent appearances, it's very striking how helpless this story makes them. They're trapped in the city, they draw their power from its metal floors by static electricity and their conflict with the Thals has clearly worked itself out to a kind of stalemate. They're a very long way indeed from the universe-conquerors seen in almost all their later appearances. The practical problems that made them figures of fun in later episodes, most obviously through the old joke about how they can climb stairs, are here consciously-chosen design points. The city (again designed by Cusick) is a deliberately Dalek-centric environment, with controls shaped to be manipulated by their sucker-arms and lifts everywhere in place of stairs.

Indeed, to push the argument further, the Daleks and the Thals present two alternate worldviews that stand in obvious contrast to each other. The Thals are, above all, 'natural'. They live in the jungle, in harmony with the planet's environment. They do not attempt to fight it or control it. (Their cloaks resemble the leaf patterns of the jungle, and especially early in the story they are presented as emerging from the forest and returning to it without being seen.) At the other extreme, the Daleks have created an environment for themselves that's nothing but artificial, right down to the machines they have placed their bodies in. Placed in this planet's environment without any knowledge of it, the Doctor and his companions have to decide which side they're on, or which set of values they agree with most.

It's a rigged debate, of course, most obviously when you consider how the script sidesteps the question of why only Daleks were mutated by the radiation but not the Thals. The Thals are not perfect. The script argues that they have to learn to use violence in extreme cases for self-defence. But they have a sense of history, and reverence for their planet and they're willing to befriend the Daleks, a trust which the Daleks are unwilling to return. The crucial difference between the two is that the Thals do not wish to control or conquer the Daleks. The Daleks, on the other hand, decide to detonate a bomb that would wipe the Thals from the planet, and so they must be stopped.

It's often asserted that the Daleks are a fictionalisation of the Nazis, and that's certainly a parallel that can be seen in later stories. In this one, though, the analogy only works clearly in two respects. First, there's a scene in which the Daleks raise their sucker-arms to signal assent to a command, an obvious reference to the Nazi salute. And their ideas of purity do lead them to the conclusion that the impure, that is, the Thals, should be removed from their planet. They are certainly not, however, the universe-conquerors of later stories. Rather, for this time only, they are the Thals' mirror image, and the story is about the argument between what their two societies represent.

The story is also, as I suggested earlier, one that shows very visibly the programme establishing a tone for itself. There are some scenes here that would seem hugely out of place even a year later, let alone five or ten. Most prominently, the Doctor is shown as selfish, narrow-minded and manipulative. This would not last long. Even by the time of the Daleks' next appearance, in November 1964, he was much more directly heroic.

What has lasted, of course, is the Daleks themselves. Many reasons have been put forward for why they became so embedded in the popular imagination, their voices, their design, the ease with which they could be imitated in play-ground games. (There's also their scope for being joked about; for many years, their inability to climb stairs would be a standard trope for comedians.) If I had to put forward one guess, though, it would be that they appealed to chil-dren so much because they were in a sense childish. That is, they embodied some of the less appealing characteristics of children. Quite apart from their cruelty, the Daleks represent above all a *retreat*; you can debate whether this was a retreat from reality, or just from their bodies. But they shut them-selves away in their shells, in their city, away from contact with the outside world. And from that position, they get to rain down destruction on the world that's rejected them. What child wouldn't like to play at doing that, if only for a while?

As the Daleks lasted, of course, so did the series as a whole. As time has gone on, their values have been seen not as the opposite to the Thals, but the opposite to the Doctor's. That process, of each being defined in terms of what the other is not, is one that's worked out through future stories. But if there's a single image to take away from this story, it's of one of the show's first attempts at model work. For its time, the vista of the Dalek city that the time travellers see early on is extraordinarily well-executed. Its spires and domes do look like a city of the future, and more importantly, it looks somehow out of place among the surrounding mountains. Wherever they go in future, the Daleks will impose their Dalek-ness on places they don't belong in, as I'll discuss in Chapter 13, where the next Dalek we see rises from the Thames.

THE CYBERMEN I (1966–75)

There's a sense in which the premise underlying the Cybermen is very close to that of the Daleks. The two have always been viewed as the most popular *Doctor Who* monsters, and they have appeared in the series far more often than competitors such as the Ice Warriors or Sontarans. So the obvious question is whether the Cybermen's success derives from the appeal of the things they and the Daleks have in common.

The Cybermen are first introduced in Hartnell's last story as the Doctor, *The Tenth Planet*+ (1966), written by Gerry Davis and Kit Pedler. That story is mostly set at a multinational base in the Antarctic that is used to monitor and control space flights. It's set in the near future, although the emphasis on manned space flight was very topical when the story was first broadcast. The Cybermen's presence is signalled by an energy drain that affects communications and the presence of a new planet in the sky with strangely familiar landmasses. When the Cybermen arrive at the base, they explain that this is their home, Mondas, Earth's 'twin' planet. One of them then describes how they came to be:

> We are called Cybermen…We were exactly like you once, but our cybernetic scientists realised that our race was getting weak…Our lifespan was getting shorter, so our scientists and doctors devised spare parts for our bodies until we could be almost completely replaced…Our brains are just like yours, except that certain weaknesses have been removed…You call them emotions, do you not? (*The Tenth Planet*, Episode 2)

So the Cybermen, like the Daleks, are presented initially as creatures that have retreated from their humanoid form into a mingled biological/mechanical nature. In both cases, this robs them of qualities that are seen as essential to humanity. The difference is that, with the Cybermen, this lack is described from the start as covering *all* emotional life. The Daleks are perfectly capable of seeking revenge, or kindling hatred. The Cybermen, at least in theory, are not.

Kit Pedler, the Cybermen's co-creator, was also involved in the TV series *Doomwatch*, whose warnings about the costs of rampant technology seem more relevant as time goes by. He was also a qualified doctor, and it seems that the material about how the Cybermen evolved as a logical extension of 'spare part' surgery came from him. Of course, the theme of humans replacing their bodies, and so their emotions, with mechanical parts was not a new one in science fiction. C L Moore's 'No Woman Born' (1944), which takes on this theme, is one of the most famous stories in the genre. But it was given added topicality in the 1960s by the beginnings of transplant surgery for hearts and other vital organs, as well as the development of devices such as the pacemaker.

In appearance, the Cybermen are, as it were, 'men-in-monster-costumes', but at least in this case that fits the story of how they came to be created. Their bodies and faces are covered in cloth or metal, they have elaborate chest units that seem connected with their breathing and handles emerge from their ears to loop round to their foreheads. Their design changes in subsequent stories, in particular, their helmets change quite a good deal, but these overall features remain constant. The same is true of their voices, which vary but are usually more affectless and mechanical than those of the Daleks.

The Tenth Planet ought to be a momentous story in *Doctor Who*'s development. Quite apart from the Cybermen's debut, the first regeneration in the series' history, from Hartnell to Troughton, is a superb coup of special effects at the very end of the story. And the topicality of the rocket programme story, and the presentation of the Antarctic base as multinational, had no parallels in the series' earlier history. Unfortunately, at least in retrospect, most of these opportunities are squandered. The Cybermen become dull, stereotyped villains, the base ends up populated by one-dimensional national stereotypes and, perhaps most surprisingly to the contemporary audience, the Doctor's regeneration has nothing to do with the story itself. Hartnell simply announces that 'This old body of mine is wearing a bit thin' and, once in the TARDIS, collapses and changes into his new incarnation. Departing Doctors nowadays are buried under the weight of flashback sequences or vastly heroic, universe-saving exits, so this hardly seems a fitting send-off for *Doctor Who*'s first star.

For the purposes of this book, though, the use of the Cybermen is what's most interesting. They made subsequent appearances in *The Moonbase+* (1967), *The Tomb of the Cybermen* (1967), *The Wheel in Space+* (1968), *The Invasion+* (1968) and *Revenge of the Cybermen* (1975). Not all of these, it has to be said, are terribly distinguished adventures, and several use the Cybermen simply as generic invaders rather than playing on what is distinctive about them. *The Moonbase*, for instance, is almost a straight replay of *The Tenth Planet*, with an isolated high-tech base under siege. The main difference is that the base is on the Moon rather than the Pole. *The Invasion* contains some memorable set pieces, such as the advance of a squad of Cybermen down the steps by St Paul's Cathedral. It is, however, most notable for its depiction of their human ally, Tobias Vaughan. As played by Kevin Stoney, he is one of the finest villains ever to grace the series, switching from oily charm to furious rage in a second. And *The Wheel in Space* is another base under attack story, though (so far as one can judge from the surviving footage) one that makes successful use of the Cybermen's ability to frighten by lurking silently in dark corners.

The two remaining stories do advance the Cybermen's mythos in various ways, sometimes to their benefit, sometimes not. *The Tomb of the Cybermen* is set on the planet Telos, many years after the Cybermen had supposedly vanished. A team of archaeologists from Earth have come to Telos to investigate the supposed 'burial place' of the Cybermen, where they hid themselves away many years before. Just as the Doctor and his companions land on Telos, the archaeologists uncover the main door to the underground tombs, and they are about to enter them. The Doctor, interestingly, does not discourage them, although it's plain that he realises how much danger they are in. Indeed, *The Tomb of the Cybermen* is the best surviving showcase for one of the most distinctive aspects of Troughton's performance as the Doctor. Most of the time, his Doctor appears to be disorganised, scatty and a little clueless; only at moments of critical importance, or when alone with his companions, does he reveal how sharp he really is. One of the archaeologists' group, Klieg, has been funding this expedition with an ulterior motive. He is a member of a group called the 'Brotherhood of Logicians', who believe that they could find powerful allies in a revived race of Cybermen. So, once the expedition enters the main chamber of the tombs, he uses the controls to revive the sleeping Cybermen. The Doctor ostentatiously defers to Klieg ('I do love to see the experts at work') until the tombs are opened.

Although *The Tomb of the Cybermen* has many flaws, the sequence that follows, the climax to the story's second episode, is one of the finest Doctor Who had produced up to that point. The tombs themselves are an almost vertical structure, arranged into five tiers, each of which carries several cells containing a Cyberman – as Klieg says, 'like a gigantic honeycomb'. Once the controls are activated, the Cybermen awake and break out of their tombs, descending the ladders at either side of the tombs to surround and tower over the Doctor and the archaeologists. Finally, they open the central tomb on the bottom level, revealing a Cyberman taller and more formidable even than the others. This is the Cybercontroller, their leader, and he announces to the humans, 'You belong to us. You shall be like us.' The credits roll.

The Tomb of the Cybermen is, therefore, the story that first exploits fully the potential in the idea of the Cybermen for body-horror. The idea of being converted from human into mechanical form carries an obvious charge of horror. Even if the process itself could not be shown in a children's series like *Doctor Who*, that perhaps adds to the thrill. Over the story's two remaining episodes, one of the party is indeed partly converted, and the story's climax depends on whether he will end up siding with his human or mechanical aspect. So, like *The Daleks*, *The Tomb of the Cybermen* ends up as an argument between two points of view, the 'human', emotional one and the Cybermen's pure logic. Klieg obviously wants to identify himself with this latter side. But it's interesting how the story shows Klieg, in a number of ways, as being *really stupid*. He's so blinded by his belief in the infallibility of logic and the idea that the Cybermen will see him as a kindred spirit that he doesn't even begin to entertain the obvious alternative: that the Cybermen will see him as not very different from the other humans. They don't see him as a potential equal or ally but another creature to be converted and subjugated. So *The Tomb of the Cybermen* is, as much as anything, about the danger of making deals with the devil.

So far as a consistent chronology of the Cybermen's evolution can be worked out, which is not an easy task, *Revenge of the Cybermen* takes place some time after *The Tomb of the Cybermen*. There has been some kind of human-led war against the Cybermen, resulting in their almost complete defeat and retreat to Telos. This is the story that introduces their supposed weakness, an aversion to gold. (The pretext given is that gold dust, being resistant to corrosion, fatally clogs the Cybermen's chest units.) So the band of Cybermen encountered are, as the Doctor describes them, 'nothing but a pathetic bunch of tin soldiers skulking about the galaxy in an ancient spaceship'.

Revenge of the Cybermen is, in fact, another base-under-siege story, at least initially. The appeal of this kind of format for *Doctor Who* is obvious. A story can be presented on a limited number of sets, with a clearly defined and limited cast. The base in this case is the Nerva Beacon, a space station orbiting Earth. Via a human collaborator, the Cybermen disable the crew with a virus and intend to use it as a base to launch an attack against Voga, a wandering asteroid with huge resources of gold. The reasons for the Cybermen's hatred of Voga are obvious, and we discover that there are also intensely fought politics among the humanoid Vogans about how they should deal with this threat.

The Cybermen are unquestionably at their least impressive in this story. This is partly because they have had a sudden, arbitrary weakness introduced for plot convenience. They are also, played as nothing more than robots who shout a lot. Their original rationale, which made them so distinctive in stories like *The Tenth Planet* and *The Tomb of the Cybermen*, has been almost entirely forgotten. When they returned several years later, both their appearance and their outlook would have been rethought thoroughly.

One final thing about these early Cybermen adventures is worth noting. In *The Tenth Planet*, the various Cybermen are given individual names. This is not repeated in any of their subsequent stories. Cybermen may be identified by their role, 'Cyber Leader' and the like, but not by anything that would give them individuality.

This is important because one of the central questions raised by the way *Doctor Who* (and other narratives) present monsters is the issue of essentialism. That is, how much does 'X is a Cyberman' define what X is? How much is X able to break free from its nature as a Cyberman to assert its own individuality? Clearly, the point of the Cybermen is that they're stripped of individuality by the very process that creates them. So one might regard the individual names in *The Tenth Planet* as a misstep, especially since it serves no real purpose in the story. However, there's a larger question here. Essentialism is the point of view that says that for any class of entities there are certain properties all those entities possess. So 'all elephants are grey' is an essentialist statement. In some cases, essentialist habits of thought are necessary for survival.

'All cars have the potential to seriously injure me if they hit me at speed', for instance. However, when applied to groups of humans, essentialism has other names, such as prejudice or racism.

The problem here is that monsters are presented on *Doctor Who* as races, as classes of creatures. Only in some cases does a monster break free from its essential monster-ness and exercise a choice. There's only one case in the TV series in which a Cyberman does this; see Chapter 23. Is there, then, a sense in which the very idea of 'a race of monsters' instils a dangerous habit of thought? That habit is the idea that you can judge the whole nature of a given race by encountering just a few of them. The central question is that of choice. Cybermen may not have a choice about their nature, but the humans they deal with do. Humans, or human-equivalents, are clearly the characters in Doctor Who that the audience are meant to identify with. One of the most consistent themes of the series is showing those human characters the cost of their choices. (I can't, for instance, think of any character in the series' history who betrays their fellow humans and survives to the end of the story.) Given such a range of human experience in the nonmonstrous characters it depicts, and, especially recently, such a good record in depicting the future as not just being populated by white males, you can certainly argue that *Doctor Who* has done more than its share against racist habits of thought. If the Cybermen are robbed of their ability to choose how they act, that almost seems like a kind of original sin for them. The real crime is not the things that they do, but the fact that they are Cybermen at all.

THE SONTARANS (1973, 1975, 1978, 1985, 2008, 2011)

There's a sense in which the Sontarans could almost be regarded as an average *Doctor Who* monster, with all the criticism that implies, but for two things. The first is, as with so many other of the most memorable *Who* creatures, the extent to which their creator Robert Holmes imbues them with far more life and culture than they need to fulfil their plot function. The second is a superb coup in their design, revealed at the end of the first episode of their debut story, *The Time Warrior* (1973). The story begins with two separate plot lines. In the Middle Ages, a spaceship crashes in a wood near a castle held by a brigand called Irongron. Irongron ventures into the wood to see what has happened and meets a strange helmeted warrior from the spaceship. This creature, a Sontaran named Linx, explains that his craft needs repairs and that, in exchange for shelter from Irongron, he will provide the human with new weapons. Linx does not reveal his face. He is short and squat, his silvery helmet almost hemispherical. Meanwhile, in the twentieth century, the Doctor investigates the disappearance of scientists from a research establishment and finds that Linx has been dragging them back in time to help with the repair of his ship. The Doctor takes the TARDIS back to the Middle Ages to find what has been happening to the scientists and soon tracks down Linx at Irongron's castle. Hiding from Linx in a courtyard, he sees the Sontaran remove its helmet and reveal a head of the same shape, leathery, hairless and neckless.

The Sontaran design was one of many created in this period by a designer named John Friedlander, who was also responsible for the Sea Devils (Chapter 11), the Vogans (Chapter 8) and the original Davros mask (Chapter 16). But Friedlander's contribution is only part of the story here. Holmes's script has much more to it than I've described. There is a subplot in which Linx constructs for Irongron a robot warrior to fight his battles for him. The Doctor's companion, Sarah Jane, tries to teach the women she encounters in the Middle Ages something of twentieth century feminism. And the Doctor introduces a little anachronism by inventing and using some primitive 'flashes and bangs'.

There's also, as I mentioned, a thoroughly thought-through culture for the Sontarans. They are a clone race, designed and bred for war. They're engaged in what the Doctor later calls an 'interminable' war with the Rutans, a species that makes its only appearance in *Horror of Fang Rock* (1977). They receive their energy from their ships through a 'probic vent' in the back of their necks. This is their only weak point; a blow there can stun them. And they have a single-mindedly martial culture. Death is glorious if found in battle. The probic vent is not a weakness because it forces them to face their enemies, and so on.

Linx's motivations in the story are also rather unusual. He's stranded far from home, and in another circumstance the viewer might almost feel pity for him. But he simply wants to get away from Earth, and back to the war, as soon as possible. Everything else is incidental, though he seems to take a certain paternal pride in Irongron's bloodthirstiness. The most distinctive thing about this Sontaran, apart from his appearance, is his singlemindedness. For that alone, *The Time Warrior* is one of the most memorable of Jon Pertwee's stories as Doctor. It also, more or less singlehandedly, invents a subgenre within the series of the 'pseudo-historical': stories which take as a given known historical events or settings but add science-fictional elements to them.

It was perhaps inevitable that subsequent stories featuring the Sontarans by writers other than Holmes were less interesting. *The Sontaran Experiment* (1975) immediately follows *The Ark in Space* (see Chapter 15). The Doctor and his companions travel to a far-future Earth supposed to have been devastated by solar flares. They find a small number of humans leading a scavenging existence. Some, however, are being captured and tortured by a Sontaran scout, Styre, who is there to assess the resistance of humans to various kinds of mental and physical trauma. He is the advance guard for a fuller Sontaran invasion.

The one thing worth noting about Styre is that the writers equip him with a very distinct sense of sadism. He clearly enjoys inflicting torture, to the point where he ignores a recall from his commanding officer so that he can continue his work with the humans. It's an interesting hint that the Sontaran's purity of focus on war and conquest can go too far, and indeed work against their goals. But it's not explored any further – *The Sontaran Experiment* is only a two-episode story – and neither is the Sontaran culture. The Doctor defeats Styre, bluffs his commander into thinking that all humans are ferocious warriors and so postpones the invasion.

Sadly, the Sontarans' appearance in *The Invasion of Time* (1978) makes them even more generic monsters. This is a six-episode story set on the Doctor's home planet of Gallifrey, and the first four episodes are fascinating. Unfortunately, the Sontarans show up at the end of the fourth episode. Up to that point, the story has been concerned with the threat of an invasion of Gallifrey by a race called the Vardans. In an early scene, the Doctor pledges his co-operation to them, and for several subsequent episodes there's a genuine question: Has the Doctor 'gone bad' and sold out his people? For once, Tom Baker's performance in these episodes has moments of great subtlety, as does that of John Arnatt as his main Time Lord confidant, the Doctor's former teacher, Borusa. It is, of course, a huge bluff on the Doctor's part. He needed to gain the Vardans' confidence in order to defeat them, and having done so exploits his knowledge of them to expel them from the planet.

When the Sontarans arrive, their commander, Stor, reveals that they had been using the Vardans as puppets. They needed to have the force field around Gallifrey lifted so that their ships could land. The last two episodes of the story might politely be called a runaround, with the Sontarans pursuing the Doctor and his companions both in the corridors of Gallifrey and the corridors of the TARDIS. Stor is eventually killed by the Doctor using a 'Demat Gun', a kind of ultimate weapon that removes forever all traces of the victim. But neither Stor nor his troopers have enough personality or distinctiveness to be at all memorable. Even Stor's incongruous Cockney accent just looks like a bad production decision rather than anything illuminating his character.

That point about distinctiveness, though, does raise one interesting issue about the Sontarans. In the last chapter, I touched on the question of monsters and essentialism, and the idea that monsters seemed not to be able to escape from their monster-nature. With the Sontarans, though, their clone nature does give a coherent reason for this. Creatures with the same genetic makeup will arguably be much the same. (Though this has been disputed by scientists recently. See Richard Lewontin's *The Doctrine of DNA* [2001].) So the Sontarans play, among other things, on the idea of what war does to people, that it reduces soldiers to dehumanised instruments of a larger purpose. Sontarans may rejoice in their nature, but it makes no less terrifying the idea of an army of identical soldiers with one purpose in mind.

Robert Holmes returned to writing Sontaran stories with *The Two Doctors* (1985). This was, however, one of his less distinguished efforts, at least partly because he was writing to an externally imposed specification. His script needed to include the presence of the Second Doctor, Patrick Troughton, in addition to the then-current incumbent, Colin Baker. It had to include the Sontarans, and it also needed to make use of foreign location filming, in this case in Seville, Spain.

The story's central thread is a reasonably common one for *Doctor Who*, the attempt by creatures other than the Time Lords to acquire or develop time travel technology. *The Time Warrior* showed the Sontarans had a primitive version of this already. In *The Two Doctors*, they seek to acquire the very much more sophisticated device developed by two scientists called Kartz and Reimer. The story begins with the Second Doctor and his companion, Jamie, arriving on the far-future space station where the Kartz-Reimer module is being developed. They meet with Dastari, the scientist overseeing the project, and attempt to persuade him to put a hold on the research. Because they are acting on instruction from the Time Lords, Dastari sees their intervention, not unreasonably, as patronising paternalism. But this is soon a moot point. There is a Sontaran attack on the space station, the Doctor is captured and he, Dastari and the Sontarans end up in Spain with the Kartz-Reimer module. Along with them are two representatives of the Androgum race. The Androgums are famous for their fondness for food and ability as cooks. ('Androgum' is an anagram of 'gourmand'.) One of the Androgums, Shockeye, served as cook on the space station, and in many respects displays the primitive nature of the species. At one point, he's shown biting into a rat. The other, Chessene, has been 'augmented' by Dastari to give her very much greater intelligence, and it's plain that she also has ambitions to make use of the Kartz-Reimer time travel machinery. The Sixth Doctor arrives in this situation, at first attempting to find out what has happened to his earlier self. He eventually finds his way to the Spanish villa where Dastari and his group are working, rescues the Second Doctor and defeats both the Sontarans and Chessene. The Kartz-Reimer machine is destroyed, yet another instance of scientific overreaching being punished and normality is restored.

Sadly, the Sontarans in *The Two Doctors* are a shadow of their former selves. Physically, they are unimpressive. Their masks are clearly loose-fitting and rubbery, unlike the implacable solidity of Friedlander's masks for Linx and Styre. They often end up playing second fiddle to the other characters, particularly Chessene (played by Jacqueline Pearce, who was so memorable as Servalan in *Blake's Seven*.) And, as in *The Invasion of Time*, the things that are unique about them are hardly used in the story.

When the Russell T Davies-led revival of the series returned to the creatures, with *The Sontaran Stratagem/The Poison Sky* (2008), it was plain that, as with the Daleks and Cybermen, the production team had gone back to first principles in rethinking what made them effective as monsters. Though the resulting rethink wasn't as radical as for those other two monsters, the resulting story did very visibly benefit from it.

For a start, the Sontarans' masks were redesigned, and the more flexible faces that resulted gave the creatures an expressiveness they had never had before. The new series' more generous budget also allowed what had never fully been seen previously: the Sontarans involved in a full-scale battle. The story intelligently picks up on the Sontarans' use of cloning technology by introducing a clone of the Doctor's companion, Martha. The production also used a piece of fan-lore that had never quite been articulated in the series: that the Sontarans' home planet was a high-gravity world, and so the creatures were much shorter than humans. By casting actors only a little taller than five feet as the creatures, they were given a distinctiveness they might otherwise have lacked.

The story, by Helen Raynor, is set on contemporary Earth, the same Earth that had suffered in quick succession invasions by Slitheen, Sycorax, Cybermen and so on in earlier stories. Its first premise is that a new device called Atmos has been introduced to reduce the toxic emissions from car exhausts. Many cars are now fitted with the Atmos system, and it seems to be unambiguously beneficial. The system was developed by a teenage prodigy called Luke Rattigan, who runs an academy for similarly gifted young people. Rattigan is revealed early on to be in the employ of the Sontarans, who have a ship orbiting Earth. Their plan, however, takes rather longer to reveal. They want to transform Earth's atmosphere so that it will become a suitable breeding planet for Sontarans. Rattigan believes that the Sontarans will reward him for his treachery by giving him and his hand-picked students a new world where they can begin a life free of interference from the mundane world. Of course, he is being duped by the Sontarans, and he is ultimately abandoned by his students. As a result, he has a change of heart in the last minutes of the story and winds up destroying the Sontarans along with himself.

In a sense, this latest Sontaran story is a fairly standard invasion-of-Earth romp. The treatment of the Sontarans, though, helps to elevate it above the norm. As I've said already, their appearance and numbers are more formidable than in any previous appearance. There are also some interesting additions to their mythos. They are given, for instance, a war-chant not unlike the 'haka' used by New Zealand rugby-players. Their commander, Staal, is given some lines which test to destruction the Sontarans' fondness for war. He describes himself as Staal the Undefeated. (Presumably, if he ever became Staal the Defeated, he'd be so mortified that he'd also be Staal the Dead.) His second-in-command, Skorr, is shown having the same lip-smacking delight in destruction that Styre had in *The Sontaran Experiment*. The design work, too, is of a high standard. The distinctive, golf-ball shaped ships that have been a feature of Sontaran stories since *The Time Warrior* are here shown as part of a larger scheme of Sontaran technology. It's never been so easy to believe in these creatures as having a unified culture and outlook on the world.

The Sontarans make three final, cameo appearances. The first is in *The End of Time* (2009–10), David Tennant's last appearance as the Doctor. After the main action of the story is complete, the world has been saved but the Doctor knows he is dying. He goes on a kind of 'farewell tour' in the TARDIS before he regenerates, visiting each of the companions who travelled with him and, in various ways, saving them. In the case of Martha, who was travelling with him in *The Sontaran Stratagem*, and her husband Mickey, he saves them from attack by a Sontaran. Just as the alien is about to fire on Martha and Mickey, the Doctor hits it on the probic vent with a big hammer. The creature falls to the ground, and Martha and Mickey look up to see how they have escaped death. It's a comic moment, with the Sontaran used almost as a punchline. The second is in *The Pandorica Opens/The Big Bang*, the finale of the 2010 season (see Chapter 1). The Sontarans appear as part of the alliance of monsters conspiring to lock the Doctor into the Pandorica. Their commander only has a few lines, but the Sontarans' distinctive appearance makes them stand out from the crowd of other monsters. The third is in *A Good Man Goes To War* (2011). The Doctor recruits a Sontaran nurse who owes him a debt to help him rescue his companion, Amy Pond. Again, here, the effect is comic. Steven Moffat's script portrays the Sontaran as a permanently grumpy healer who saves peoples' lives and then pledges to kill them when he meets them on the field of battle. To return to the point I made at the start, this would not have been possible without the culture that Robert Holmes laid out more than 35 years before. It's one of the unique strengths of *Doctor Who* that it can draw on such a wealth of history.

THE SLITHEEN (2005)

The Slitheen were the first major new aliens to go in front of the cameras in the 2005 revival of *Doctor Who*. Although they appear in *Aliens of London* and *World War Three*, the fourth and fifth episodes to be broadcast, the filming took place in the first block of shooting along with *Rose*, as discussed in Chapter 1. So it might be expected that they would set the agenda for the kind of creatures that would appear in the new series, and they do.

The first thing to say about these episodes, written by Russell T Davies, is that they are so full of decoy plotlines that the wrongness of expectations is almost their central subject. The story begins with the Doctor and Rose landing back in London after their first few adventures. The Doctor tells Rose that she's only been away for 12 hours. However, on returning to Rose's mother, they soon find it's been 12 months, and that Rose has been listed as a missing person. Just as the Doctor and Rose are sitting on the roof working out the consequences of this mistake, they see a spaceship flying low overhead and heading for central London. There, it crashes into Big Ben and splashes down in the Thames. The authorities soon surround it and take the pilots to a nearby hospital for examination. The Doctor takes the TARDIS there and discovers that the aliens are augmented pig hybrids, frightened by the strange environment they find themselves in.

Meanwhile, the Prime Minister has 'mysteriously disappeared' and the power structure at Downing Street has been taken over by a range of seemingly minor political and military figures, who share only two characteristics – that they're quite fat and prone to flatulence. The Doctor is eventually summoned to a summit at Downing Street to discuss the menace, but this is a trap. One of the fat politicians we've seen earlier begins to open a zip in his forehead and reveals himself as a Slitheen, a green humanoid alien with sharp claws but childlike, fluting voices. The Slitheens' attempt to kill those at the summit doesn't quite succeed. The Doctor escapes, and eventually winds up bargaining with them from inside the Cabinet Room. There, one of the aliens reveals that 'Slitheen' is not the name of their race but of their family. They are exiles from the planet Raxacoricofallapatorius, and their presence on Earth is not aimed at conquest or enslavement but simply to break it up for scrap. Only the Doctor's last-minute intervention, summoning a military missile strike against Downing Street, is able to avert their plans.

The most obvious thing, to me, about these episodes, is Davies' fondness for subverting the expectations viewers might have. For much of the first episode, for instance, it seems that the crashed Thames spaceship and the creatures inside it will be the real threat. The fact that they're a decoy only emerges gradually and as a result of the Doctor's investigations. Most other people in the country won't have grasped this, and indeed this allows Davies to indulge in some heavy-handed satire in the second episode, when one of the fat politicians comes out of Downing Street to spin a further lie about 'massive weapons of destruction'. Similarly, one expects the Slitheen (like almost every other monster in the story's history) to be a race intent on conquering the Earth. And when Davies does, later, produce an alien race intent on conquering the Earth, he subverts their 'normal monsterness' in other ways: see Chapter 18 on the Sycorax.

The Slitheen could, then, be seen as aliens that are cobbled together out of several bits, each designed to produce individual moments of memorable television. They have claws so that they can be a threat when they're chasing our heroes down corridors. They have babyish faces and voices because that's a slightly creepy trope. They masquerade as human authority figures because that gives children an idea to play with the next time they encounter a fat relative or teacher. They're green because, well...green is the default colour for monsters. (There is, doubtless, a whole separate book to be written on why that's the case, with excursions into humans' associations of green with reptiles, moss, slime, mould and so on.)

In the 1980s, the writer Bruce Sterling coined the idea of 'eyeball kicks' as something that marked out good science fiction. Eyeball kicks were individual details or ideas in an SF story that wound up being striking or memorable. I've argued elsewhere (Sleight, 2006) that the problem with pursuing eyeball kicks, as Sterling does in his novel *Distraction*, is that it tends to produce works that are full of local incident and colour but that don't hang together as coherent stories. The same, arguably, is true of Davies' writing for *Doctor Who*. The question is whether it matters as much. *Distraction* is an attempt to describe, fully and coherently, a near-future America. It matters a great deal if Sterling comes up with a radical idea and then doesn't follow through its implications. *Aliens of London* is meant to be a kinetic, colourful part of a prime-time SF series whose main job is to get relatively young children watching. Hence, the flatulence. Adults might sneer at this or suggest it was 'dumbing-down' the programme, but anecdotally it's one of the things that children remembered most about the story.

The idea that the Slitheen are a family rather than a race is an intriguing one, but it's hardly followed through in the story. Its main purpose, I'd argue, is to send viewers the message that *this is not quite the Doctor Who you remember*, and its corollary, *so you'd better keep watching*. As much as monsters may have a back story or culture within the series, it's equally important to remember that they were designed by a writer who wants people to watch a story. Steven Moffat's monsters are an even more extreme example of this. See Chapter 2 on the Weeping Angels.

Davies then gave the Slitheen an encore in *Boom Town*, the eleventh episode of the 2005 season. This is a very different story than their first appearance, more personal and intimate (and, as Davies has said, less expensive to make). The premise is that Blon Fel-Fotch Pasameer-Day Slitheen, one of the leaders of the group seen in the earlier story, escaped the explosion of Downing Street. She got herself to safety with an emergency teleport, and in a few intervening months, has installed herself as Mayor of Cardiff. There she plans to build a nuclear power station that's secretly designed to melt down and open up the rift in space-time beneath Cardiff. With a hidden 'extrapolator' device, she hopes to escape Earth, riding the waves of the explosion to a new home.

Again, expectations are upset in *Boom Town*. The Doctor and his companions capture Blon (as she's known) early on in the story; the question then becomes what to do with her. The Doctor's preference is to return her to her home planet, where she will be dealt with by their own legal system. But she will almost certainly be put to death, and asks the Doctor whether he is willing to be complicit in her execution. The Doctor seems to have no qualms, and indeed fulfils Blon's 'last request' by taking her to dinner at a favourite restaurant of hers in Cardiff Bay. There, Blon attempts various tricks to defeat the Doctor, but all of these fail. Only when they return to the TARDIS does the threat become more serious. Blon has used the extrapolator to trigger an earthquake in Cardiff, the foreshadowing of a far greater disaster when the rift will crack open. For good measure, she takes the Doctor's companion, Rose, hostage. The threat is averted when Blon looks into 'the heart of the TARDIS', a brilliantly glowing light, and, in effect, a deus ex machina. She is reduced back to an egg, ready to be born and have another chance. The Doctor can return the egg to Raxacoricofallapatorius, where it can be nurtured perhaps better than the first time around.

So *Boom Town* is, unashamedly, a relatively small story, but as so often with Davies' writing, the heart of it is in the emotional moments it captures. In an early scene, Blon realises that she cannot kill a female journalist who has stumbled on to her plan about the nuclear plant. This change from the self we had seen in the earlier story is a huge one. It's not quite that Blon has escaped her nature entirely, but the information that the journalist is pregnant does stop her in her tracks. The core of the episode is the long scene in which Blon and the Doctor eat dinner together. Here Davies does introduce a few new characteristics for the Slitheen; in dire need, they can exhale poison gas or fire darts from their fingers. But the main argument conducted here is about the rights and wrongs of Blon's and the Doctor's lives. The Doctor, as he does so often in the series, is setting himself up as judge and jury over the deeds of others. Even if he doesn't carry a gun, he's as responsible for their deaths as if he did. Blon is just the latest instance of this happening. On the other hand, there's no question that Blon has been directly responsible for deaths; we've seen them in the earlier story. But it's clear, to go back to the point about essentialism, that she isn't inherently evil. She had, and has, a choice. However contrived the ending is, it makes the point that if she starts over again she may have a different and better life.

So the Slitheen may, as I suggested earlier, be a kind of compilation album of good bits that might make up a frightening monster. But in this episode, Davies does give them a complexity they didn't have otherwise. He elevates them, in fact, to the status that humans have always had in *Doctor Who*: as creatures who can *choose* good or evil, and who should be judged accordingly.

THE SILURIANS AND THE SEA-DEVILS
(1970, 1972, 1984, 2010)

Throughout this book, the assumption is that monsters often 'stand for' something – that they can be taken to represent some limited aspect of human nature, and that in that limitation is often found both their strength and the source of their defeat. That argument is certainly easy to make with, say, the Sontarans or the Cybermen. With the eponymous creatures from *Doctor Who and the Silurians* (1970), I want to make a slightly different argument. Despite the Silurians being human-sized reptiles with a third eye that can be used as a kind of heat-vision, they most closely resemble humanity as a whole. The story's disturbing impact can be traced to the strong sense that, were we in their position, we would not do very differently.

It has to be said that the story is not perfect. At seven episodes, it is much too long for the material it has to use, and it spends several episodes dabbling in suspense before revealing the real threat. It also has incidental music, using medieval instruments such as the shawn, that many people find distracting and obtrusive. And its setting, a scientific research base under mysterious attack, is hardly original for the series. Malcolm Hulke, its author, is one of the crucial figures who shepherded the programme into the Jon Pertwee era; his novelisation of the story is also of great interest, as I'll argue later.

The story begins in some caves adjoining the base, which we later find out is located in a part of England called Wenley Moor. Two cavers are attacked by a mysterious, unseen creature which, at least from the noises it makes, we judge to be huge. The Doctor is summoned by UNIT to help investigate the research centre's recent troubles: unexplained power loss and a high incidence of mental breakdowns. The centre contains a prototype cyclotron, a device which its controllers hope will lead to the creation of a new and more efficient form of nuclear power. (The parallels with the research establishments in *Inferno* and *The Claws of Axos* don't need to be pointed out, though in this case, the story is not easily readable as a dire warning against humanity overreaching.) The head of the research centre, Dr Lawrence, is actively hostile to UNIT's intervention and defensive about its state. However, his deputy, Dr Quinn, is rather friendlier, and he gives the Doctor an introductory tour of the facility. Also important in the story is the centre's Head of Security, a former army officer called Major Baker, who initially suspects that the problems can be blamed on a deliberate programme of sabotage.

The Doctor first visits one of the cavers attacked at the beginning of the story. He was originally in a coma, but now sits in his room, seemingly not responsive to human speech, but sketching strange designs on the walls. These include what seem to be representations of the caves and reptilian creatures living within them. Following this hint, the Doctor ventures into the caves and is attacked by the same creature that menaced the cavers, and which we can now see is a Tyrannosaurus Rex. But before it can strike him, it appears to be called off by a strange groaning noise. The Doctor returns safely to the base, and returns with a much larger search party including the Brigadier and Major Baker. During this expedition, they are again menaced by the dinosaur, and

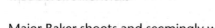

Major Baker shoots and seemingly wounds a creature that he sees in the caves. It seems to have a human shape.

Soon enough, we see from this creature's point of view its escape onto the moor. Wounded and frightened, it hides in a barn. Meanwhile, we see Quinn making his way through the caves on his own. He demands from unseen observers the knowledge he says he was promised. He is told that he must rescue the injured creature from the barn. He does so, narrowly missing the Doctor, but arousing his suspicion. When the Doctor goes to Quinn's cottage on the moor, he finds it uncomfortably hot, 'like a reptile house'. He becomes more suspicious after breaking into Quinn's office at the research base, where he finds a globe showing the continents in their position millions of years ago, during the Silurian era. He returns to Quinn's cottage determined to confront him, but finds him dead and instead confronts the wounded reptile whom Quinn had been sheltering. Though the creature walks upright, and from its gestures seems intelligent, it flees.

At this point, almost four episodes in, the premise of the story finally becomes clear. The Silurians were sentient creatures who inhabited Earth millions of years ago. They feared their civilisation was threatened by an impending asteroid collision, and so built themselves subterranean shelters across the globe. The expected cataclysm did not happen, though; the asteroid settled into orbit as Earth's moon. The Silurians slept on until this particular base was awakened by the activities of Dr Lawrence's research centre. They are responsible for the power losses, and the dinosaur kept in the caves is a creature from their era under their control.

At this point, the story takes two tracks. The first is a relatively conventional one of threat and jeopardy. The Silurians have created a virus which, they believe, will wipe humanity from 'their' planet. The second is rather subtler, and involves the Doctor's attempts to negotiate with them and see whether they and the humans can co-exist peacefully. He points out that there are vast areas of the planet, particularly those with warmer climates, which are basically inhospitable to human life. The Silurians, he suggests, might be able to live there.

So the story inverts the usual moral schema of *Doctor Who*. Instead of a human-inhabited world being under threat from external invasion, here we have a situation in which humans could be seen as interlopers in the Silurians' world. (In Hulke's novelisation, *Doctor Who and the Cave Monsters*, there's a prologue not featured in the TV adaptation, told from the viewpoint of the Silurians. However, it takes quite some time for it to become apparent that it's not a human telling the story, and so the reader's sympathies for the reptiles are reinforced from the start.) Like humans, the Silurians have different shades of opinion about how to deal with the problem. Some see potential in the Doctor's idea of co-existence with humans; others are more belligerent, and engineer the release of the virus.

Perhaps predictably, the end of the story returns to the status quo rather than leaving these questions open. The Doctor finds an antidote to the Silurian virus and has it distributed before the disease can do too much damage. A Silurian attempt to use the research base's reactor to power another weapon of theirs backfires, and they retreat to their caves. And, finally, as the Doctor is driving away, he sees a series of explosions on the moor. The Brigadier has followed orders from above to destroy the Silurian base.

The story raises the question of what a happier solution to this impasse would be. Could humans and Silurians really co-exist? Would the implicit diminution of human sovereignty over the planet be something people would tolerate? There would certainly be benefits from such co-existence. It's clear that the Silurians' technology is far in advance of the humans'. But equally, there's almost an admission of guilt inherent in any acknowledgement of the Silurians' case. It's significant that the Doctor is the person who goes furthest towards meeting the Silurians' concerns: he arguably has less stake in, or less possessiveness about, the Earth.

As I said at the start of this chapter, the Silurians are so memorable as monsters because, once one gets past their initial 'monster-ness', it's clear that they're neither thoughtless, evil or of uniform views. They accept reason and argue with each other, just as humans do. They may in the end be driven to evil acts, like the release of their virus. This, however, is clearly a last step and a victory for extremists in their group rather than moderates. It's difficult to imagine that humans would act any better or any differently in their place. The one thing that's clear from the story is its condemnation of violent means, whoever they're used by.

The series returned to this concept on two more occasions. *The Sea Devils* (1972), also by Hulke, was a re-run of a very similar set of ideas, the differences being that the Sea Devils were ocean-dwelling cousins of the Silurians, and in this instance were being manipulated by the Master. If nothing else, they were superbly designed creatures (again created by John Friedlander) whose turtle-like masks were in fact worn as hats atop the actors' heads so that they towered even over Pertwee. Friedlander's designs made a virtue of necessity. Since the latex he used wasn't able to articulate smoothly with the actor's features, neither the Sea Devils nor Silurians moved their lips in any normal way as they spoke. This greatly added to their strangeness, and the sense that they were radically different from the humans they were dealing with.

Given what I argued above about the condemnation of military values in *Doctor Who and The Silurians*, it's interesting that *The Sea Devils* was made with the co-operation of the Royal Navy, and features a great deal of their equipment in action. There are scenes set aboard ship, the use of a diving bell, travel in hovercrafts and a final assault on a naval base. If nothing else, it's the sort of spectacle that would have been immensely appealing to the eight-year-old boys in the audience.

However, design aside, there's no question that the Sea Devils are less impressive figures than the Silurians. They are effectively duped by the Master, and although the story reruns the debate about how they might survive in a human-dominated world, it's not conducted with the same intensity as first time round. The viewers, as it were, know what the answer will be. In the end, a Sea Devil attack is thwarted, their base is destroyed and the disturbing question of humans needing to cede part of their planet to a species with a better claim on it gets ducked.

Warriors of the Deep (1984) was set a century in the future, in an underwater 'Sea Base' controlled by one of two global power-blocs and poised, as in 1984, to unleash global destruction through intercontinental missiles. The Doctor and his companions, Tegan and Turlough, land on the Sea Base more or less by accident, and are immediately suspected as saboteurs. In fact, the Base is already under heightened pressure. Missile launch requires the intervention of a surgically modified 'sync operator' whose brain can interface directly with the base's computers. The main sync operator, Lt Michaels, has died from a freak electrocution before the action of the story starts, and his deputy, Maddox, is plainly unprepared for the responsibility. In fact, two of the base's staff are spies for the opposing power bloc and have been engineering the incremental breakdown of its systems. (*Warriors of the Deep* is often cited as a story in which the design and lighting let down the intentions of the script. The Sea Base is clearly intended to be rusting and decrepit, yet the set designs render it as pristine, white and brightly lit.) The Base's level of alert is heightened by an unexplained blip on its scanners, which prompts a dummy 'missile run'. Maddox faints during this, and Nilson and Solow persuade the Base's commander to release him into their care for 'reprogramming', ostensibly to make him more suited for his job.

The 'blip' is in fact a submarine Silurian craft. The three Silurians aboard are heading, firstly, to revive a cadre of Sea Devils to assist in their plan. The story does posit an interesting rationale for the two working together. There is a kind of caste system whereby the Silurians are the rulers or 'executives' while the Sea Devils are especially skilled in warfare. Soon enough, a full-scale invasion of the base by Silurians and Sea Devils takes place. This takes up most of the story's duration, with various complications. The Doctor attempts first to hold back the invaders and then to negotiate with the Silurians. But the reptiles are set on their plan to release the Base's missiles, so provoking a war to destroy humanity, and leaving the planet free for their race to reclaim. This is stopped by the Doctor only at huge cost in lives, Silurian, Sea Devil and human, and in the end he and his companions are almost the only survivors. The Doctor's last act is to block the Silurians' planned missile launch. As he finishes, he looks round at the bodies strewn across the Base's command deck and says, 'There should have been another way.'

So *Warriors of the Deep* did return to the first story's theme of caution about the worth of military might. It's clear that the presence of the Sea Base's fearsome weaponry only increases the chance of misunderstanding and conflict with the Silurians. It also allows them to feel that annihilating humanity with its own weapons is almost fitting. *Doctor Who* has always been notionally a 'pacifist' series, with the Doctor's condemnation of violence acted out in his unwillingness to carry a gun. But in few other stories is that principle put at the heart of the story. Certainly, the deaths of many characters and extras are far more telling than usual. And *Warriors of the Deep* adds something to the argument of Hulke's two earlier stories. It doesn't just suggest that violence is not the way to deal with a question like this, it argues that violence will tend to breed violence and make things more unstable for everyone. The Sea Base's missiles are just the most obvious symbol of this. If the Silurians are, as Hulke's original novelisation argues, just humanity in a different guise, it's a rather sobering thought that humanity is shown throughout these stories as only being able to respond to violence with violence.

The Silurians, though not the Sea Devils, returned once again in *The Hungry Earth/Cold Blood* (2010). This story, by Chris Chibnall, is very visibly a reprise of *Doctor Who and the Silurians*. An isolated human research establishment delves underground and, in doing so, disturbs Silurian sleepers. The establishment comes under attack, the Doctor enters the fray, attempts to mediate between the humans and the reptiles and fails. That said, the story does bring to bear the resources of twenty-first-century *Doctor Who* on these monsters. So, for instance, we see for the first time a full-scale Silurian city. We're given a fuller sense of the structure of their society, stratified into specialists like scientists and soldiers. We see, as we never have done before, the beginnings of a proper negotiation between humans and Silurians on how the planet might be shared between them. As in all the previous stories, though, no rapprochement is possible and aggressive urges on both sides cause the negotiation to fall apart.

Independent of its originality, this is a story in which a single production decision undermines, for me, at least, its goals. In the first three stories considered here, the Silurian and Sea Devil masks were relatively inflexible. As a consequence, they did not articulate as human faces do, and so it was an authentically estranging experience to see voices emerging from them. By 2010, though, prosthetics were capable of being moulded to individual faces and so responding much more closely to an actor's facial expressions. (For another example of this, compare the difference between the 1970s versions of both Davros and the Sontarans and their revivals in 2008.) In the case of the Silurians, though, the redesign simply means they look like actors with green prosthetics stuck to their face. The alien-ness and otherness that was so much a part of their previous appearances were gone.

For this reason, the Silurians in this new story simply aren't as striking or scary as in the original, despite all the extra resources that the new *Doctor Who* can throw at them. There are, no doubt, new stories to be told about them: what would, for instance, a society look like in which humans and Silurians co-existed? The issues raised by the idea of the Silurians are some of the most fascinating and nuanced the series has discussed. How much of an obligation do humans have to the Silurians? Who is the coloniser here, and who the indigenous people? How can very different worldviews come to cooperate? It may simply be, though, that stories this complex are not easy to tell well in a forum like *Doctor Who*.

THE HAEMOVORES (1989)

One of the commonest tropes in horror stories is the sins of the past coming back in dreadfully altered form. *The Curse of Fenric* (1989) is very much in this mode, although with a distinctly science-fictional twist. Of all *Doctor Who* stories, it's one of the most densely packed with action, ideas and references to other tales.

In fact, in common with a number of other stories around this period, its ambition exceeded what could be shown onscreen. More material was shot than could be fitted into the original four 25-minute episodes. The current DVD release presents two versions: the one originally transmitted, and an expanded version with extra footage and updated effects, presented as a 'movie' rather than with episode-breaks. It's to this extended edition that I'll refer in what follows.

The setting of the story is an army base on the English coast in World War II. The Doctor and his companion Ace land there, seemingly at random, and the Doctor manages to bluff their way into the compound by faking a letter from Winston Churchill. Inside the base, they meet a scientist named Judson who is working to crack German cyphers using a primitive computer. Judson is confined to a wheel-chair, but otherwise seems closely modelled on the real-life scientist Alan Turing (Hodges, 1983). Judson is fascinated that a young woman like Ace has (for her, given her 1980s background, routine) knowledge of computers.

At the same time, a party of Russian soldiers is landing on the shores near the base in inflatable rafts. For reasons unexplained at this point, we're shown viewpoint shots of the rafts from underwater, and one of their number is found on the beach unconscious. Their mission appears to be to break into the base and capture Judson's 'Ultima' machine, but their arrival is already anticipated and the base's guards are primed to look out for them.

A third thread follows activities in the village near the base. Some teenage girls are there, having been evacuated from London, as is a church whose crypt contains ancient Viking inscriptions. Judson is investigating these inscriptions, trying to use the same cryptographic techniques as he does on the German cyphers.

From this point, a sense begins to gather that events in the story are foreordained. The church is built on old Viking graves, and a little exploration in its graveyard reveals that many of the village's founders have Viking names. The vicar, who has succeeded his father and grandfather in this post, knows something of what the Viking inscriptions mean and has a larger collection of them transcribed by his predecessors. They say, among other things, 'I know now what the curse of Fenric seeks: the treasures from the silk lands in the east. I've heard the treasures whisper in my dreams. I've heard the magic words that will release great powers.'

Ace goes down to the beach with two teenage evacuees, but unlike them, obeys an injunction from the Doctor not to swim in the water. The evacuees are, like the Russian rafts, seen from underwater in viewpoint shots. Back at the base, the Doctor is allowed into another circle of secrets by its commander, Millington. He has in fact been ordered to allow the Russian troops to steal the Ultima machine, but this is a trap. The machine contains a phial of toxin which will be broken once a certain word is transmitted – in this case, the word is 'love'. Millington demonstrates the potency of the toxin on a couple of chickens, and tells the Doctor he sees it being used to speed the end of the war, whether in bombs on Dresden or Moscow. The base has vast stocks of the toxin, seemingly in anticipation of this plan.

About 40 minutes into the story, it shifts from being one of anticipation to action. The two evacuees whom Ace had befriended venture into the water and are dragged under by unseen forces. They then emerge, seemingly transformed, and beckon one of the Russian troops in like Sirens. He is grabbed by hands from half-seen creatures and dragged under too. These creatures are the Haemovores, and from this point on they become increasingly aggressive in their ventures beyond the water. They are dressed in clothing from all periods, but share common characteristics. They have claw-like hands, and faces that are pale (in the early stages of their lives) or, later, light blue and encrusted with what seem to be barnacles. They feed on human life, specifically, as the name suggests, on their blood.

So the Haemovores are, in a sense, vampires. But their myth has been intriguingly reimagined here. They can be repelled by faith or belief rather than by symbols such as the cross. So, in one memorable scene, they confront the vicar. Because he has doubts, very human doubts, about the reality of what he preaches, they are able to overcome him. But, in a later scene, they are held back by the Russian captain, who does have faith in something: the revolution in his country. It doesn't matter that we, as viewers, might think that a dubious thing to have faith in, belief is all. (Ironically enough, *The Curse of Fenric*'s original broadcast was in the weeks around the fall of the Berlin Wall.)

The question then is: What exactly are the Haemovores? The Doctor explains that they are 'what humanity evolves into thousands of years from now'. Their form has been warped by the toxins and poisons released into the environment by the species, toxins just like the ones Millington is planning to unleash on the Germans. So the further question is: How did a contingent of these creatures from the future come to reside under the water by this base for at least a thousand years? That question is left on one side for a while as a full-blown Haemovore assault on the land begins. The action that follows takes up much of the middle third of the story. Ultimately, many of the base's personnel have been captured and converted to Haemovores (again, just like vampires).

At a certain point, it becomes clear that there are two puppet masters at work here, the Doctor and the creature known as Fenric. Fenric is the embodiment of some kind of primal evil that emerged during the Big Bang. It encountered the Doctor many years before, and challenged him to a game of chess. The Doctor won, and Fenric's spirit was sealed in a metal flask. It's this flask that is the 'treasure from the East' referred to in the inscription, and that's found behind a wall beneath the church.

Soon enough, the flask is opened, and the spirit of Fenric takes over Judson. He stands from his wheelchair. In the melee of events that follows, the fourth and final episode of the original broadcast, perhaps the most important are a pair of conversations. The first is between the Fenric-possessed Judson and the largest and oldest of the Haemovores, 'the Ancient One':

> **DOCTOR JUDSON:** At last, another of the wolves of Fenric decides to show up and play his role.
> **THE ANCIENT ONE:** My world is dead.
> **DOCTOR JUDSON:** Hardly a great loss, if you're the best evolution could manage. This is the twentieth century. It doesn't become your world for a long time yet.
> [And, later]
> **DOCTOR JUDSON:** Take the poison. Carry it to the ocean. Release it in the waters.
> **THE ANCIENT ONE:** And the other Haemovores?
> **DOCTOR JUDSON:** You know how to kill them.

Later, the Doctor has a similar conversation. In part, it answers the question about how the Haemovores got here, and what they've been doing. More to the point, it can also be seen as the Doctor persuading the Ancient One to his side.

THE DOCTOR: I've been waiting.

THE ANCIENT ONE: You know me?

THE DOCTOR: Thousands of years in the future, the Earth lies dying. The surface just a chemical slime. Half a million years of industrial progress.

THE ANCIENT ONE: I am the last. The last living creature on Earth. I watched my world dying with chemicals, and I could do nothing. My world is dead.

[And, later]

THE DOCTOR: You're very patient. Carried back thousands of years in a time storm, to ninth-century Transylvania, and waiting till now.

THE ANCIENT ONE: Without the flask, I was trapped.

THE DOCTOR: Oh yes, the flask. I trapped him like an evil genie.

THE ANCIENT ONE: Only he can return me to the future.

THE DOCTOR: And so, like a faithful servant, you follow the flask.

THE ANCIENT ONE: A merchant bought it from Constantinople. I followed him through Europe. I followed the Viking pirates who stole it, and I followed it here.

THE DOCTOR: Another of Fenric's games. He carries you back in a time storm, to destroy the Earth's water with chemicals. To destroy your future. Think of it, your Earth, your world, dying of a chemical slime. This act will be the beginning of your end.

So, among other things, this is an instance of *Doctor Who* providing (pseudo-)scientific rationalisations for myths. If the Haemovores showed up in ninth-century Transylvania, their presence could easily have been transformed into the original vampire myths. The difference is that, unlike source materials such as Dracula (Stoker, 1897), the Ancient One seems receptive to the idea that death might be desirable.

The idea of having a 'good death' comes up more than once in *Doctor Who,* not least on occasions (such as *Planet of the Spiders* [1973] and *The End of Time* [2009–10]) when the Doctor has to regenerate. In this instance, the Ancient One does not respond to the Doctor's suggestion, but there's a clear sense that the thought is in his mind. So, when the Doctor comes to his final confrontation with Fenric, now in the body of the Russian soldier Sorin, it's the Ancient One who finally breaks the impasse. He forces Sorin into a sealed chamber, and releases the toxin to kill both of them but no one else.

So, at the end of the story, all the Haemovores seem to be dead. Most of them are killed by the Ancient One's intervention, and the Ancient One himself has committed a kind of suicide. What's left are the stories constructed about them, the vampire myths that the story alludes to and revises. (It's worth remembering that, in *Dracula*, the vampire comes ashore at Whitby, like the village shown here a North Sea port.) But vampires can carry a wider range of resonances too, whether in the currently booming 'paranormal romance' genre or in stories like those collected in Ellen Datlow's *Blood is Not Enough* (1989). Datlow's anthology in particular argues that vampirism should be understood first of all as something psychological, not physical. Vampires are creatures that are incomplete, and they carry out a never-ending quest to fill that gap by draining life from those around them. The twist that *The Curse of Fenric* puts on this idea is that the vampires are us – that we're reduced to vampirism by what we're doing to our planet. These vampires are at the opposite pole from, say, Edward Cullen in Stephanie Meyer's *Twilight* books. There's no otherworldly glamour to them, no sense of the allure of eternal life. There's just emptiness, and waiting for the release of death. *The Curse of Fenric* is justifiably celebrated as one of the richest *Doctor Who* stories. It should also be seen as one of the grimmest.

THE DALEKS II (1964–74)

The Daleks was a huge success, one that guaranteed the future of *Doctor Who* in the short-term. The creatures' return was, therefore, guaranteed before too long. Over the following years, an appearance by the Daleks became almost an annual feature of the show. They featured in *The Dalek Invasion of Earth* (1964), *The Chase* (1965), *Mission to the Unknown*+ (1965), *The Daleks' Masterplan*+ (1965–66) (all starring Hartnell's Doctor), and then *The Power of the Daleks*+ (1966) and *The Evil of the Daleks*+ (1967) with Troughton. A break followed, principally because of Terry Nation's attempt to market the Daleks independently in Hollywood. When this failed, they returned in the Pertwee stories *Day of the Daleks* (1972), *Planet of the Daleks* (1973) and *Death to the Daleks* (1974).

It has to be said that several of these are fairly unremarkable productions. The Pertwee Dalek stories, in particular, are often full of science fiction clichés and predictable plotting. Indeed, the stories that seem most interesting now are, sadly, those in which most episodes are lost from the BBC archives: the one-episode *Mission to the Unknown* and its 12-episode sequel *The Daleks' Masterplan* and the two Troughton stories.

Perhaps significantly, Terry Nation had relatively little hand in writing these, whereas he did have a hand in the mediocre Pertwee tales *Planet of the Daleks* and *Death to the Daleks*.

For a sense of the strengths and weaknesses of Nation's approach to his creatures, *The Dalek Invasion of Earth* is the obvious place to start. For the first episode, the Doctor and his companions are almost on their own, exploring the area around the TARDIS's landing-place at the edge of the Thames in London. Despite their location, the place is eerily silent, and the city seems to be mostly deserted. They manage to establish that the year is 2164, but before too many conclusions can be drawn from this a Dalek emerges from the Thames and confronts the Doctor.

By this point, some of the Doctor's companions have been drawn into the resistance movement, and it's through this thread that the back story is explained. Some years before, humanity suffered a plague that killed many and split humanity into fragmented communities. The Dalek spaceships arrived relatively recently and exploited this weakness. The Daleks are making London a centre of their operations because they have a major project nearby, in Bedfordshire. There they are drilling deep into the Earth's core for some unknown reason. Only towards the end of the story is this explained: the Daleks hope to remove Earth's magnetic core and replace it with a kind of engine that will enable them to steer the planet wherever they want in the universe.

This last idea seems, now, so completely absurd that it's hard to focus on the story's many strong points. The scenes among the human resistance, for instance, are gritty and have a strong sense of risk and danger. They point to the obvious parallel to be drawn with this London under Dalek occupation: the experience of World War II. Part of the imagery of shattered buildings comes from the Blitz, of course, though given budgetary restrictions, there actually aren't many vistas showing the damage the Daleks have wreaked on the city. The resistance material is more relevant, though. The many heroic stories of resistance in France and elsewhere are here transferred to Britain. And, in that scenario, it's far easier than in their debut to identify the Daleks with the Nazis. They are ruthless, single-minded and place science at the heart of achieving their dreams of power and conquest.

As I've suggested, though, the story has plenty of weaknesses, both in its scripting and its realisation. Its one major revision to the Daleks' nature is that it removes the helplessness that I remarked on in their debut story. There they were confined to their metal city, drawing their power from static electricity carried through the floors. Here, they can go anywhere, and the seeds of their future existence as universe-conquerors are sown.

The next Dalek story, *The Chase* (1965) is exactly what its title suggests. The Daleks discover time travel technology and use it to pursue the Doctor through time and space. Their eventual defeat, by a similar race of creatures called the Mechanoids, is spectacular, but the series of set pieces that lead to it are slackly scripted and directed, and add very little to our idea of the Daleks.

Mission to the Unknown+ (1965) is unique in the series' history. It's an episode without any participation by the Doctor or his companions. In it, a 'Space Security Service' agent named Marc Cory finds, on the planet Kembel, a gathering organised by the Daleks and including many other alien species. The Daleks have a plan to conquer Earth, and Cory leaves a recorded message about this in the jungle outside the Dalek base before he is killed. This message is found and followed up in the sequel, the 12-episode *The Daleks' Masterplan+* (1965–66). The central plot device is an invention called the Time Destructor, a weapon with which the Daleks believe they will be invincible. This requires the use of the element Taranium, which can only be found in our solar system. It is supplied by Mavic Chen, ostensibly 'guardian' of that solar system, but in reality a power-hungry megalomaniac who has allied himself with the Daleks. Only three episodes of this story survive, but they reveal that Chen was perhaps its most interesting feature. He is played by Kevin Stoney with the same wit and flair that he brought to a similar role in *The Invasion* (see Chapter 8).

The Power of the Daleks+ (1966) is, perhaps, one of two or three stories in *Doctor Who*'s history in which the series' survival was most at stake. It was Patrick Troughton's debut as the Doctor following William Hartnell's regeneration at the end of *The Tenth Planet*. Because it was the first time this had occurred, there was very real doubt about whether this new man really 'was' the Doctor. As a result, many of the Doctorish duties of investigation and exposition are taken over by his companions, Ben and Polly. The action takes place on the planet Vulcan, where a human colony has discovered a crashed Dalek spaceship. This has been discovered by the colony's scientists, and the Daleks are being tentatively reactivated. They seem, for most of the story, to be acting completely out of character: they are keen to serve the scientists of the colony and show no public signs of their old ruthlessness. The story is a huge exercise in irony, with the viewers (and the Doctor and his companions) knowing much more than the colonists.

So, for most of its length, *The Power of the Daleks* is a gratifyingly risky story. Not only is the Doctor not behaving as he did in the past, neither are the Daleks. Only at the end of the penultimate episode are their true intentions finally confirmed, as they stream out of their ship, intent on slaughtering the humans. There is, I think, no other story in the series that so effectively demonstrates the creatures' sheer cunning, their willingness to deceive to reach their goals.

The Power of the Daleks was principally written by David Whitaker, the series' first script editor. He also provided *The Evil of the Daleks+* (1967), Troughton's final Dalek story. (Indeed, as Terry Nation was seeking to create other series which featured the Daleks, it seemed for a while that it might be their very last appearance in the series.) It begins innocently enough, with the TARDIS being abducted in contemporary London. Soon enough, though, the doctor and his companions find themselves in Victorian London, where two scientists named Maxtible and Waterfield have made a Faustian deal with the Daleks. They assist the Daleks, and coerce the Doctor to assist in isolating and making transmissible the 'human factor' which the Daleks are seeking. They want to isolate and analyse this factor because they believe it has been the root cause of their many defeats. After some trials, this is achieved, and the action shifts to Skaro, where the Doctor encounters for the first time the Dalek Emperor, a vast immobile creature towering over the main control room. Eventually, a civil war ensues between 'normal' Daleks and some infected with the human factor, resulting in the destruction of the Dalek city. The Doctor escapes with his companions and looks down on the resulting chaos, muttering 'The final end...'.

Of all stories currently incomplete in the BBC's archives, *The Evil of the Daleks* is the one I personally would most value having returned. Only the second episode (of seven) survives, and the audio and photos that survive of the remainder promise much. There is, for instance, the irresistible sight of Daleks gliding down the halls of a Victorian mansion, or of human-infected Daleks indulging in childlike bouts of play. There is some surviving footage of the final battle between Daleks of different factions, but what's particularly interesting about the story is how it's structured as a continuous crescendo to that explosive end. As Wood and Miles argue (2006b), the scale keeps increasing. It looks first like a story set on contemporary Earth, then a Victorian romp, then a return to Skaro. There's a superb moment in the penultimate episode when the Doctor first encounters the Dalek Emperor: the Emperor, voiced magnificently by Peter Hawkins, announces that 'the experiment is over'. It signals that the rest of the story is going to take place on an even bigger stage than before. Of all the stories Whitaker contributed to the series, this is surely the finest and most ambitious.

The Evil of the Daleks is, without saying so, an examination of the ideas of essentialism I've talked about earlier. In its worldview, 'human nature' or 'Dalek nature' are things that are capable of being captured and encoded by science. Once they have been encoded, they then become transferable. 'Evil' in this context is not just an abstract noun, but a substance in the world just like mercury or oxygen. (One of Whitaker's amusing foibles as a writer is his fondness for investing a few substances like mercury or static electricity with enormous, almost supernatural power. *Evil of the Daleks* has, as Wood and Miles demonstrate, a similar fascination with the odder byways of Victorian science and alchemy.) So *The Evil of the Daleks* is a story that could be told with almost any other monster in place of the Daleks; but it could not be told so well. The Daleks by this point had established themselves as the *Doctor Who* monster above all others, so a story that investigated and questioned their nature had a certain inevitability. On the surviving evidence, it was also one of the greatest *Doctor Who* stories.

There was then an interval of five years before the Daleks reappeared, in *Day of the Daleks* (1972). This story, by Louis Marks, was originally conceived without their presence, and their late addition is evident; they are scarcely central to the plot. In a sense, it's a story that plays with the same issues as *Inferno* and other parallel world stories: how choice works, and how individual human actions affect history as a whole. It's partly set in contemporary Britain, and partly a few centuries in the future, where the Daleks have invaded and established a harsh regime together with their servants, the Ogrons. As in *The Dalek Invasion of Earth*, there is a human resistance force in the future. They have determined that the events that enabled the Dalek take-over were set in motion in the earlier timezone, with a peace conference run by Sir Reginald Styles. They send a fighter back in time to try to assassinate Styles, and so avert the invasion. This mysterious incursion is what draws the Doctor in, and ultimately takes him forward in time to the Dalek-dominated future.

So this story, in fact, goes further than *Inferno*. Not only do human choices matter, but they can generate many possible worlds, and time travel allows those worlds to be changed. The Daleks, as I say, are less important to the story than the dilemmas about individual choice that it exposes. In any case, for this first appearance in colour on television they are not looking at their best. There are only three Dalek props, and their voices sound squeaky and unconvincing. It's significant, also, that this is the first time onscreen that we see the Daleks with a race of soldiers working for them, as if on their own they weren't a big enough threat.

After this slightly uneasy reappearance of the Daleks, *Planet of the Daleks* should have been a far grander return. It was written by Terry Nation, his first story for the series since *The Daleks' Masterplan*, and also featured the return of the Thals. The Daleks, in fact, make brief appearances in the previous story, *Frontier in Space*, manipulating events along with the Master to try to provoke a galactic war. The Doctor resolves the diplomatic tensions in *Frontier in Space*, and heads off to the planet Spiridon to find the Dalek army that's supposedly poised to take advantage of the chaos.

Planet of the Daleks, unfortunately, ends up relying on a number of clichés that were common to a lot of Nation's work. Despite the title of the story, the build-up in *Frontier in Space*, and the extensive prepublicity, the revelation that the Daleks are present on Spiridon is presented as a supposedly shocking cliffhanger to the first episode. There's also a jungle filled with potentially dangerous creatures (as seen in both *The Daleks* and *The Daleks' Masterplan*), a friendly but strange indigenous species, and a presentation of the Thals as bland do-gooders. Planet of the Daleks also, frankly, has far too little plot for its six episodes, with many arbitrary obstacles being put in the Doctor's path before he finds the Dalek army. It also adds nothing to the Dalek mythology, unless you count having a Supreme Dalek that's gold and slightly larger than the others are. The days of the David Whitaker stories challenging assumptions about the Daleks are long gone.

The same is true of the following year's story, *Death to the Daleks*, also by Nation. The one change it offers is that both the Daleks and the Doctor are relatively helpless in it. Both find themselves stranded on the planet Exxilon, victims of a power drain caused by a mysterious city built there many years ago. The Daleks have to replace their energy weapons with machine guns, and conceal their weakness from the other parties on Exxilon. Both they and a human landing party are there trying to mine an ore called parrinium, which helps them create a cure to a plague afflicting both species. Once again, there's a 'shocking' first-episode cliffhanger as the Daleks arrive, a friendly native creature, and so on.

Death to the Daleks was, in other words, a thoroughly routine story, almost a parody of what might be expected from a Dalek appearance in *Doctor Who*. A change in how they were treated was clearly necessary, and it arrived in the next season – as Chapter 16 describes.

THE ZARBI (1965)

*T*he Web Planet (1965) is, to date, the only occasion when a *Doctor Who* story has featured no humanoid characters apart from the Doctor and his companions. It may perhaps say something that such an experiment has never been repeated by the series in the 45 years since. But, as with many stories discussed in this book, there's an obvious distinction to be made in considering it: between the ambitions set out by the script, and how those ambitions are translated onto the screen.

The story begins with the TARDIS being forced to land on the planet Vortis. This is a desolate place, with thin air, barren rocks and no vegetation. We see four different alien races on this world. The first to be shown are the Zarbi, human-sized but ant-like in appearance, and capable of communicating only by a kind of high-pitched buzzing. The second is a race of similarly mute 'venom grub' creatures. The third are the Menoptra, butterfly-like original inhabitants of the planet. Related are the fourth, a subspecies of Menoptra called the Optera, who have become adapted to life underground.

The bulk of the story is taken up with the Doctor and his companions' alliance with the Menoptra as they battle against a creature called the Animus, which arrived on the planet some years ago. The Animus, seemingly one of a kind, exerted a malign influence over the creatures of Vortis, controlling the previously docile Zarbi and so driving the Menoptra from the planet. They lived in exile on one of its moons, and are only now trying to return. The revolt against the Animus eventually succeeds, and the Menoptra's life on the planet is restored as it was before.

Even more than with other black and white stories, *The Web Planet* is one in which the viewer has to make allowances. It is undeniably slow and hampered hugely by the constraints of the tiny studio it was made in. In a world where viewers are used to vast computer-generated vistas, the tricks used in *The Web Planet* – forced-perspective sets and lunar landscapes that sound audibly wooden – are, very visibly, just tricks. Moreover, the lack of other human characters points up a real problem that many monsters have. They are, compared to humans, incredibly inexpressive. Once in a while, as with the Daleks or the Cybermen, this limitation becomes an advantage. But here, most of the nonhuman speaking parts are for the Menoptra. Their masks simply do not allow for the same range of expression as a human face. It's particularly problematic that characters who are supposed to have shifting affections and feelings do not have visibly mobile eyes. The eyes are, after all, so often the most telling sign in the human face.

All this is not to say, of course, that the production team didn't anticipate these problems. Indeed, quite apart from the expense of all the alien sets and costumes, the evidence is that they thought long and hard about how to depict these aliens. They employed Roslyn de Winter, a trained dancer, to work with the various alien actors on creating distinctive and appropriate movements. The script also goes much further than any before or since in thinking through what a fully alien culture would be like. Again, though, much of this effort ends up seeming a bit silly. The Menoptra move, by and large, in a slow and dreamlike way, perhaps to suggest that they aren't used to the gravity on Vortis. But they end up looking like actors *pretending*, unconvincingly – there's no real sense that their waving their arms around has any functional purpose. It also, unfortunately, emphasises that the wings attached to their backs are just painted plastic. It's simply not possible to imagine these creatures flying. The Menoptra's ritualised, halting speech is more effective, though perhaps only because it's similar to that used by many other monsters in *Doctor Who*.

Rather more interesting is the way in which, particularly late in the story, the Menoptra outline their deeper cultural understandings. They have an elaborate religious or societal outlook with light at its centre, and much of what the Animus has done can be understood as a kind of perversion of the true light of Vortis. (There's a separate, obvious reference to be picked up here, the two other senses of the word animus. The first, is the sense in which it means a strong dislike and the second, the sense it takes in the psychology of Jung, as the masculine part of the individual's psyche. That said, the Animus' voice is provided by a female actor, and so any attempt to give it those overtones is somewhat muffled.) In any case, the Menoptra's speech is threaded through with references to this metaphysical concept. For instance, the moon they have been exiled to is a 'dim' place, and this lack of light is associated with their being unable to fly there, presumably because the atmosphere is too thin. Similarly, almost the worst of the Animus' crimes seems to be that it has some Menoptra stripped of their wings. The restoration at the end of the story, with the Animus destroyed, is explicitly a return of both light and flight.

The Zarbi, though wordless, are at least as interesting as the Menoptra. First, their design is truly effective, closely resembling stylised ants. Their huge, bulbous eyes are especially effective. The costume also manages to conceal, much of the time, that there is a human performer inside, bent over as in the back half of a pantomime horse. The Zarbi also play on a common human fascination, how strange ants are as creatures, particularly when they act collectively. It is one of *Doctor Who*'s most distinctive moments when a group of them moves in concert to, say, hold one of the Doctor's companions hostage. It's only slightly undermined by the ubiquitous cheeping sound they make, like a synthesised Tweety Pie.

So *The Web Planet* underlines one of the fundamental distinctions among monsters: between those that speak and those that cannot. There's no monster in *Doctor Who* that's made more than three appearances without being able to speak, and this probably shouldn't be surprising. Speech, after all, gives, the creature a chance to express itself fully and to argue back against the Doctor. It also gives the chance for more variety in how the creature is presented. It allows, for instance, the Daleks to put on their show of seeming subservience in *The Power of the Daleks*, or Styre to reveal his streak of sadism in *The Sontaran Experiment*. There's an obvious overlap here with histories of how humans have evolved and used language, such as Steven Pinker's *The Language Instinct*.

In the context of *The Web Planet*, speech is what marks out the Menoptra as being more intelligent than the Zarbi. The story at no point questions the idea that the Zarbi are just mindless drones, or that their chirping noise is effectively without meaning. Speech also allows the Menoptra to be presented, like the Silurians, as a society with a range of opinions (in this case about how to fight the Animus). The Animus, by contrast, is only one voice, a totalitarian one. No debate is permitted among its ant-servants. Voice means dialogue, and dialogue means disagreement. It's impossible to imagine the Zarbi speaking without imagining this story being utterly different.

THE WIRRN (1974)

I f nothing else, the experiment with the Zarbi and the Menopetra showed that insects can provide fertile inspiration for the forms that monsters might take. A decade later, the series returned to the same idea though in a very different mode. *The Ark in Space* (1975), Tom Baker's second story as the Doctor, is set on a space station where a sleeping human population has been attacked by the insect-like Wirrn.

In many respects, *The Ark in Space* represents a return to the norm for *Doctor Who*. The era of Baker's predecessor, Jon Pertwee, was premised on the Doctor's exile to Earth and his role within the 'UNIT family', frequently in defeating alien invasions. Although, following *The Three Doctors*, the exile was revoked and the Doctor given control of his TARDIS again, many of the most emblematic later Pertwee stories (*The Green Death, The Time Warrior, Planet of the Spiders*) are at least partly based on contemporary Earth. And, when Baker made his debut as the Doctor, it was the production team's choice to give him a first story that could equally have featured Pertwee. That story, *Robot*, has the Doctor collaborating with UNIT to defeat a group of unhinged scientists who have built a giant robot to carry out their wishes. At the end of the story, though, the Doctor and his companions step into the TARDIS for a first trip, and end up on the space station of *The Ark in Space*.

The story also marks the first occasion when it's possible to see some distinctive characteristics of the regime of producer Philip Hinchcliffe and script editor Robert Holmes, which was to last for the next three years. This is often thought of as *Doctor Who*'s 'gothic horror' period, and it certainly goes very much further than any previous era in displaying extremes of human emotions, and the fact that many of the Doctor's adventures will entail the kind of body-horror previously considered too intense for its tea-time audience.

The Ark in Space approaches this territory gradually. Its first sequence is a shot from the point of view of some unknown creature moving along the corridors of the Ark. It's clearly doing something to the equipment in the otherwise deserted space station, but what exactly isn't clear. The rest of the first episode is taken up entirely with the Doctor and his companions' early explorations of the Ark. Apart from some prerecorded voices played by computers, there are no other speaking parts in this first episode, yet it remains one of the most entrancing pieces of *Doctor Who* because of the sense of discovery throughout. It becomes clear that the Ark is the home for a huge number of humans frozen in deep sleep, that it's extensively equipped with defence mechanisms to prevent the sleepers from being disturbed, and that one of the defence mechanisms was sabotaged – the cables cut – before the Doctor arrived. At the end of the episode, the Doctor finds himself in one of the main sleep chambers, with the whole of Earth's natural and cultural heritage preserved in a side chamber, and delivers 'Homo sapiens: what an inventive, invincible species. It's only a few million years since they crawled up out of the mud and learned to walk. Puny, defenceless bipeds. They've survived flood, famine and plague. They've survived cosmic wars and holocausts. And now here they are, out among the stars, waiting to begin a new life, ready to out-sit eternity. They're indomitable.' And then, the episode's cliffhanger, one of the cryogenic tombs is opened, and a huge green insect-like creature falls out.

It rapidly becomes clear that this is a corpse. The Doctor begins reviving some of the human sleepers: the most prominent of them are called Noah and Vira, seemingly the leaders of this group. They are as puzzled as the Doctor by the presence of the insect-creature: it was in the berth of one of their technicians, named Dune. There is, at least, some explanation of why they are here. Some centuries ago, the Earth was threatened by solar flares with the potential to wipe out all life on the planet. So, in order to preserve the species, an old space station was retrofitted to accommodate a group of sleeping humans who would be awakened once the danger had passed. Not least of the consequences of the insect-creatures' attack on the Ark's defence mechanisms is that the sleepers have been kept in suspended animation for many more centuries than they should have been. Only the Doctor's arrival and intervention has brought about their revival.

Both are rather hostile to the presence of the Doctor and his companions, Noah especially so. They certainly don't have much time for the Doctor's cautions about the insect-creatures and what they might be doing on the station. Noah goes to what the Doctor suspects is now the core of the problem, the space station's solar stack. There he is attacked by a fleetingly-seen green creature, which leaves a trail of slime on his hand. There follows a contamination very similar to what happened with the Primords in *Inferno*, and not just in the facile sense that both are caused by green slime. Noah finds himself quickly taken over by what the contamination carries, the group-mind of the insect-creatures who invaded the ship, and who are called the Wirrn. Within a short space of time, he is transformed into one of them, although he remains capable, unlike the rest of them, of speech. But, unlike *Inferno*, for most of the third episode, we are able to follow Noah's transformation and so *The Ark in Space* becomes a kind of possession story. We are shown, in very vivid detail, Noah's progressive change into the form of a Wirrn and, in equally clear detail, the struggle between the human and Wirrn components of his mind. Indeed, this might almost have been too vivid; a scene is cut from the story in which the partly-possessed Noah begs Vira to kill him.

By the time of the story's fourth and final episode, some more of the Wirrn's life-cycle has been explained. They travel through the cold of space, finding life (such as the human sleepers) in which they can lay their eggs and reproduce. They seem to have a kind of group-consciousness: much like the Zarbi, insect life is associated with conformity. The Noah-Wirrn becomes a kind of spokesperson for the creatures, and the conclusion of the story follows a kind of process of bargaining between them and the surviving humans. The Wirrn want to continue their hatching (already well underway in the solar stack) and use the sleeping humans of the Ark for food. By a combination of argument and deviousness, the Doctor forces them instead to assemble in a rocket attached to the space station; they are to blast off and not trouble the humans any more. In the end, after the rocket leaves, it explodes. The Doctor deduces that the Noah-Wirrn, retaining some vestige of his humanity, did this deliberately.

So *The Ark in Space* is a story about whether, and how, it's possible to escape the kind of conformity that the Wirrn represent. It's not just the Wirrn, though, who have a narrow worldview. Noah and Vira too, despite all their evident intelligence, have real problems accepting the presence of the Doctor and his companions. The revived humans are all dressed in very similar uniforms, and their sleeping chambers resemble both insect-hives and the Cybermen's cryogenic chamber in *The Tomb of the Cybermen*. The difference between the Wirrn and the humans is that the humans are shown as having greater capacity to adapt and to express their individual natures. The Wirrn are also, unlike the humans, parasitic on other sentient creatures, and see nothing wrong with this. It's this, rather than any innate fondness for Earth's inhabitants, that makes the Doctor side with the humans.

For a story about insects laying their eggs in the bodies of other creatures, *The Ark in Space* is remarkably free from gore; not a single drop of blood is glimpsed in it. But it is, as I suggested earlier, full of emotional intensity. There's no

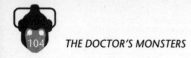

ducking the idea of bodily possession by the Wirrn, or that this could well entail the loss of one's humanity. There's also a clear sense that evolution might produce creatures such as the Wirrn quite frequently, and so that one species' needs may come into irreconcilable conflict with another's. In a sense, then, the Wirrn are cousins to the Haemovores, parasitic on other life and so need to be defeated.

THE DALEKS III (1975–88)

The five stories covered by this chapter, *Genesis of the Daleks* (1975), *Destiny of the Daleks* (1979), *Resurrection of the Daleks* (1984), *Revelation of the Daleks* (1985) and *Remembrance of the Daleks* (1988), can collectively be thought of as the Davros stories. The first of them introduces the character of Davros as the creator of the Daleks on Skaro, seemingly many thousands of years before the action of *The Daleks* (1963–64). Each of the subsequent Davros stories places this single character at the centre of events, and of the Daleks' plans. This has both good and bad effects on the Daleks' force as a televisual presence.

Genesis of the Daleks is, as comics writers would say, an origin story. It focuses far more on Davros than on his creations. The planet Skaro has been bogged down in a centuries-long war between two parties, the Kaleds and the Thals. Radioactive weapons have been used extensively, and mutations frequently result. The Doctor and his companions, Harry and Sarah, are sent by the Time Lords to intervene at this moment and place. The Time Lords fear that the Daleks might, if not checked, become the dominant force in the universe. The Doctor is, therefore, asked to try to prevent their creation or, at least, to see if he can make them into less aggressive creatures. When this idea is put to him, the Doctor accepts more or less instantly. He doesn't seem to see any moral problems with the idea of wiping out a whole race.

Soon enough, the Doctor finds his way to a Kaled scientific research bunker, where Davros is working. He is crippled and restricted to a chair resembling a Dalek base. He and his colleagues are trying to perfect the 'Mark Three Travel Machine', although it's what the Doctor and the viewers recognise as a Dalek. This will carry the mutated 'final form' of the Kaled race into whatever environments it chooses, and it will have only one goal: to secure the continued existence of that race. Here, even more explicitly than in *The Daleks* or *The Dalek Invasion of Earth*, we can see the idea of the Daleks as exploiting ideas of genetic purity, as did the Nazis. The production picks up on this, giving the Kaleds uniforms and salutes very similar to those of the Nazis. (Peter Miles, playing Davros' deputy Nyder, added an Iron Cross to his costume until he was told to remove it by the director.) We can see also that Davros is creating the Daleks in his own image, starting from the chair in which he sits. But he is going further and subjecting Kaled genetic material to chemical and radiological exposure to hasten its arrival at a final mutated form.

The story has plenty of back and forth, perhaps too much, as the Doctor, Sarah and Harry escape from one jeopardy or another, dashing back and forth between the Kaled and the Thal cities. (Interestingly, given their benign treatment in other Nation stories like *The Daleks* and *Planet of the Daleks*, the Thals are shown here as not much better than the Kaleds. The only real difference between them is that the Kaleds have a genius like Davros working for them.) But it boils down in the end to two central scenes. The first is between the Doctor and Davros in the fifth episode, the second taken up almost entirely by the Doctor in the sixth and final episode.

In the first, Davros has realised that the Doctor and his companions are time travellers and that the Doctor has knowledge of the Daleks' future history. He has therefore tortured Sarah and Harry to make the Doctor reveal how the Daleks are defeated in these future encounters. With this knowledge, he intends to redesign the Daleks to anticipate whatever weaknesses their future opponents might have exploited. Only under great duress does the Doctor comply, and soon afterwards, he finds and destroys the tape made of his 'confession'. But immediately after he finishes chronicling Dalek defeats, Davros invites him to stay and talk, 'not as prisoner and captor, but as men of science'. The Doctor puts the argument that the Daleks, as created by Davros, are evil; he responds, 'No! No, I will not accept that. They are conditioned simply to survive. They can survive only by becoming the dominant species. When all other life forms are suppressed, when the Daleks are the supreme rulers of the universe, then you will have peace.' The Doctor doesn't put the obvious counter-argument, that a desire for survival, unmoderated by anything else, can fairly be called evil. Instead, he makes a famous argument by analogy:

> **THE DOCTOR:** Davros, if you had created a virus in your laboratory. Something contagious and infectious that killed on contact. A virus that would destroy all other forms of life...would you allow its use?
> **DAVROS:** It is an interesting conjecture.
> **THE DOCTOR:** Would you do it?
> **DAVROS:** The only living thing...the microscopic organism...reigning supreme...A fascinating idea.
> **THE DOCTOR:** But would you do it?
> **DAVROS:** Yes. Yes. To hold in my hand, a capsule that contained such power. To know that life and death on such a scale was my choice. To know that the tiny pressure on my thumb, enough to break the glass, would end everything. Yes. I would do it. That power would set me up above the gods. And through the Daleks I shall have that power!

A great deal of *Genesis of the Daleks'* status as a classic stems from Michael Wisher's performance as Davros, one that, for various reasons, he did not repeat in any of the subsequent stories before his death in 1995. It's not exactly fair to say that the actors who followed him have been weak imitations of the original. As I'll discuss later, some of their performances have been fine in their own ways. But they were playing a part created so strongly by Wisher that they were inevitably in his shadow. Wisher had supplied voices for the Daleks during the Jon Pertwee era, and his delivery of Davros' lines shows this experience. When Davros is calm, the voice is high, insinuating, almost slightly wheedling. But when he becomes angry, it breaks up syllables delivered in a furious monotone – the Dalek voice in embryo. That's exactly what he does in the last speech quoted above, and as he does so, he loses control and gives the Doctor a chance to overpower him and threaten to shut down his life support systems. Though this confrontation ends in a stand-off, the point is clear: Davros, and through him the Daleks, have a kind of singlemindedness that both helps and hinders them.

Among other things, *Genesis of the Daleks* is a parable about creations outdistancing their creator. Davros is ultimately exterminated by Daleks in the bunker who have been programmed to recognise no other life form but themselves, the protocol that Davros himself hardwired into them. To have missed the implications of it demonstrates that Davros' obsession with the Daleks has blinded him to both the ethical and practical issues that their creation causes. Earlier in the same, final episode of the story, the Doctor is subjected to a test of the same faculties. He and some allies have wired one of Davros' labs to explode. It's the one in which Davros has been experimenting with the final forms of the Kaled mutations. Destroying it will set back the development of the Daleks hugely and perhaps permanently. But the Doctor hesitates before touching together the detonator wires:

> THE DOCTOR: If someone who knew the future, pointed out a child to you and told you that that child would grow up totally evil, to be a ruthless dictator who would destroy millions of lives…could you then kill that child?
> SARAH JANE: We're talking about the Daleks. The most evil creatures ever invented. You must destroy them. You must complete your mission for the Time Lords!
> THE DOCTOR: Do I have the right? Simply touch one wire against the other and that's it. The Daleks cease to exist.

Hundreds of millions of people, thousands of generations can live without fear...in peace, and never even know the word 'Dalek'.

SARAH JANE: Then why wait? If it was a disease or some sort of bacteria you were destroying, you wouldn't hesitate.

THE DOCTOR: But if I kill. Wipe out a whole intelligent life form, then I become like them. I'd be no better than the Daleks.

Like the earlier one, this debate is not concluded. Another of the Doctor's allies comes along with the news that Davros has agreed to shut down production of the Daleks. The Doctor is off the hook, even though Davros' offer is a ruse. In the end, the Daleks do remain trapped in their bunker by tunnel-blocking rubble. The Doctor speculates that their intervention may have delayed their development by perhaps a thousand years. He says in the story's final words, 'I know that although the Daleks will create havoc and destruction for millions of years. I know also, that out of their evil, must come something good.'

To me, this sounds like sophistry or denial. A thousand years of delay, if it'll really take the Daleks that long to get through a blocked tunnel, is a fraction of the time spans *Doctor Who* usually deals with. *Genesis of the Daleks* is interesting not so much for what the Daleks do, they are probably onscreen for less time than in any other Dalek story, but for its account of how something this evil can be produced by a society like that of the Kaleds, which isn't so different from our own.

Destiny of the Daleks, also written by Nation, brings the Doctor and Romana back to Skaro many thousands of years later. The planet is a ruin again, and the Daleks have returned to it to try to recover and revive Davros. They are locked in an interstellar war with a race of robots called the Movellans. Because both sides adhere to machine-driven logic, both are locked in a perpetual stalemate, doomed to anticipate and counteract the moves the other makes. They hope that Davros will be able to revise or enhance their natures so that they can defeat the Movellans. The Doctor's intervention results in the destruction of both the Dalek and the Movellan forces on

Skaro. Davros is captured and taken to Earth to stand trial for his crimes.

Like the Pertwee Dalek stories it's reminiscent of, *Destiny of the Daleks* doesn't really add anything to the Dalek mythos. It's even set in that archetypal *Doctor Who* location, a sandpit. The central premise is also surely a bit questionable. Part of the Daleks' nature from the start has been that they are not robots, but organic creatures in metal shells. They certainly exhibit emotional responses, even in *Destiny*. So the idea that they're in some sense the same as the Movellans takes some getting used to. It's also worth saying that the Daleks in this story are in worse physical condition than in any previous story, including *Day of the Daleks*. They seem like the battered props they probably were.

Resurrection of the Daleks is, to my mind, one of the 'classic' series' best directed and most atmospheric stories. However, it's vulnerable to the same criticism I made in Chapter 10 of Russell T Davies' Slitheen stories: It's a collection of individual set pieces rather than a coherent story in itself. It begins in contemporary London back streets behind Tower Bridge. A set of escapees, seemingly from the future, are gunned down by ordinary uniformed policemen and then vanish, transported back to a Dalek ship elsewhere. The Doctor and his companions soon arrive and discover that hidden at the London site are several canisters of the Movellan virus. Moreover, the London site is connected by a 'time tunnel' to a Dalek ship somewhere in the far future. This ship is on an assignment to rescue Davros from the prison ship where he has been held by humans for decades since his trial. The Daleks are losing their war with the Movellans because of the use of a virus that attacks only Dalek tissue. They want Davros to engineer some kind of cure to the virus, perhaps re-engineering them in the future.

The most intriguing notion that this story embodies is the idea of the Daleks splitting into two factions. Davros resents the existence of a Supreme Dalek and intends to put himself in charge of his creations. To fulfil this plan, he programmes two Daleks to obey his orders, and a kind of civil war begins. It's cut short by the explosion of the spaceship on which he's working, but it lays the ground for future adventures. Davros is played in this and the two subsequent stories by Terry Molloy, who does at least capture the furious rage of the original if not always the insinuating subtlety. The Doctor's role in the story is relatively minimal. He discovers the Dalek presence on Earth, travels to the prison ship, has an inconclusive encounter with Davros and gets out just before the final explosion.

If nothing else, though, *Resurrection of the Daleks* does make the Daleks unpredictable once more. The idea of the factional war among Daleks makes them more than just megalomaniac conquerors. And Davros is situated not as their unquestioned leader but as one part of a more complicated and political game.

Revelation of the Daleks is one of the series' most interesting experiments in tone, but that tone has very little to do with the Daleks, and only slightly more to do with Davros. It takes place on the planet Necros, which serves as a kind of mortuary for the galaxy's great and good. Following the events of *Resurrection* (which he survived by using an escape capsule) Davros has installed himself on Necros under the guise of the 'Great Healer'. Although he seems to be a benevolent ruler, he is actually doing two things: experimenting on the flesh of human corpses to try to breed a new race of Daleks, and using the flesh of those deemed unsuitable for this treatment as a foodstuff which he sells to fund his operations. Davros has at least got as far as creating a few Daleks from his new template; these are designed in an impressive white-and-gold colour scheme. (The idea of using humans as a food source had occurred before in science fiction, most famously in the film *Soylent Green* [1973].)

The Doctor and Peri enter this situation, in theory, to mourn the death of a friend of the Doctor's, Arthur Stengos. But there are other factions at work. A mercenary has been despatched to kill Davros, some 'grave-robbers' are investigating the true nature of Davros' work and a group of 'normal' black-and-grey Daleks soon arrive with the intention of capturing Davros and bringing him back to Skaro. The first half of the story is almost entirely build-up for what happens when these threads meet in the second half. Inevitably, there are explosions, fights and a confrontation between the Doctor and Davros. But Davros is ultimately captured by the Daleks and taken away to stand trial.

As I hinted, *Revelation of the Daleks* is a story that could almost take place without the Doctor's intervention, and much of its quality derives from some fine direction, sardonic dialogue and a sense of humour even more gruesome than that wielded by Robert Holmes. (It's also one of the most visually memorable stories because the extensive location shooting took place, quite by accident, in snow-bound landscapes that suit the new design of Dalek perfectly.) Its author, Eric Saward, has stated that much of its plot came from Evelyn Waugh's satire of the funeral industry, *The Loved One*.

Remembrance of the Daleks was the first story of the series' 25th anniversary season, and appropriately it takes in a number of references from the past. It's set in 1963 London, around the Totter's Lane junkyard in which the TARDIS was found in the very first episode of *An Unearthly Child*. The Doctor has returned to this time and place because of some unfinished business. He left in London a Time Lord device called the Hand of Omega, a 'remote stellar manipulator' used in early time travel experiments. Two Dalek factions are now seeking it to use as a weapon: white-and-gold Imperial Daleks, and grey-and-black 'Renegade Daleks'. The former are commanded from an orbiting spaceship led by an Emperor Dalek who looks very like the one in the 1960s comics and not at all like the one in *Evil of the Daleks*. Only at the end of the story is it revealed that this is actually Davros, having shed 'the last vestiges of [his] human form'.

The ideas of a Dalek civil war is very much foregrounded here. The two factions of Daleks have been subject to different kinds of genetic and mechanical augmentation. As a result, each hates the other for being, as the Doctor's companion, Ace, puts it, 'not pure in their blobbiness'. The parallels, once again, are with Nazi ideas of genetics and purity. The point is driven home by the Renegade Daleks' co-option of a racist secret society, 'the Organisation' to do their work for them. This is a 1960s London where boarding houses have signs in their windows saying 'No Coloureds', and where respectable establishment figures can say that they feel Britain fought on the wrong side in the last war.

In McCoy's period as the Doctor, the show was as political as it has ever been. (At his interview for the job of script editor, Andrew Cartmel said that his goal, if he got the job, would be 'to bring down the government' [Cartmel, 2005].) Sometimes, as in the following story, *The Happiness Patrol*, this political satire is heavy-handed and overbearing. But here, and in a piece like *Survival* (Chapter 28), points are made with concision and grace. Although it ends with the destruction of Skaro and the defeat of both factions of Daleks, *Remembrance of the Daleks* renews the creatures and restores their uniqueness. It helps that it features by far the most convincing scenes of the Daleks in battle shown up to this point. They are once again believable both as organic creatures trapped in metal shells and as conquerors of the universe. Of course, it would be more than 15 years before they returned to the screen.

THE DÆMONS (1971)

One of the axioms of *Doctor Who* is that the universe is always susceptible to rational explanation. So the Doctor is, among other things, a perpetually curious scientist, always testing his hypotheses, always deducing from the evidence around him. At the same time, though, the programme is clearly attracted to ideas of the supra-rational, like magic and myth. They make good narratives, and they tap into older reservoirs of story that viewers might half-remember. *Doctor Who*'s usual strategy, therefore, when dealing with magic or myth, is to present some initial happenings that seem to be explicable in that way. Once the Doctor starts investigating, though, he finds ways in which an original scientific explanation has been corrupted into superstition, usually over many years. By doing so, he gives himself insights, not available to those who don't share his empiricism, enabling him to defeat whatever the threat is. (It occasionally also applies this approach to that other supra-rational narrative, religion, as in *The Face of Evil* [1977]. But given the obvious sensitivities around religion, this happens much more rarely.)

Early on in *The Dæmons*, the Doctor is working on his car, Bessie (ever the practical empiricist), and we hear from off-screen the voice of his companion, Jo Grant, 'But it really *is* the dawning of the Age of Aquarius!...Well, that means the occult! The supernatural and all that magic bit.' The Doctor chastises her that the world works by rational, discoverable laws. He goes on to prove the point when his car appears to move on its own, by magic: It is, in fact, remote-controlled. Even by the show's usual standards of making the companions daffy women who are corrected by the knows-better older man (and Jo is probably the worst example in the series' history), this is a particularly egregious bit of debate-rigging. But it does at least set the terms for a tension that runs throughout *The Dæmons*: the Doctor having his empiricism tested by the suspicion that it may in fact not be sufficient.

The Dæmons is credited onscreen to the writer Guy Leopold, which is in fact a pseudonym for Robert Sloman and the show's producer Barry Letts. It's fondly remembered for a number of reasons. It marks, perhaps, the zenith of the 'UNIT family', the group of characters around the Doctor following his exile to Earth. It also features perhaps the definitive performance by Roger Delgado as the Master. And it does tap into the mythic ideas underlying its premise with skill and flair. It's especially well directed by Christopher Barry. Although the children who were *Doctor Who*'s core viewers wouldn't have seen them, the then-booming industry of Hammer horror films such as *The Devil Rides Out* (1968) are another clear influence here.

Most of the action takes place at the Wiltshire village of Devil's End, where an archaeological dig into a local mound, the 'Devil's Hump', is about to uncover what the excavators believe will be a lost treasure trove. The dig is to be televised and, in the run-up to it, there's an onscreen argument between a local 'white witch', Olive Hawthorne, and the lead archaeologist, Professor Horner. Miss Hawthorne has 'cast the runes', and predicts nothing less than the return of 'the horned one' if the dig goes ahead. Seeing this onscreen, the Doctor and Jo set off for Devil's End. Meanwhile, Miss Hawthorne tries to get hold of the local vicar, 'Mr Magister', who in fact, is the Master. The dig finally takes place (at midnight on the eve of the pagan festival Beltane), and is disastrous. As Professor Horner breaks into the burial chamber, a blast of freezing air rushes out, the ground shakes and the TV equipment is blown over. The Doctor and Jo arrive just in time to witness this, and the Doctor is frozen into unconsciousness by the wind. Meanwhile, the Master has been conducting an occult ceremony beneath the church, seemingly intent on summoning a being called Azal. As the Doctor recovers, and the rest of UNIT converges on Devil's End, a series of strange happenings take place. Huge cloven hoof prints appear in fields around Devil's End, and a 'heat barrier' surrounds the village so that nothing can get in or out. He soon encounters Miss Hawthorne, agrees with her that the dig should have been called off, but disagrees with her explanations for why. Whatever else was happening, it was not an attempt to summon the devil.

Returning to the site of the dig, the Doctor and Jo find in the inner chamber a tiny spaceship on the floor. It appears to be fixed to the floor, but the Doctor suggests that instead it weighs many tons but has been miniaturised. While they are investigating, they are attacked by Bok, a church gargoyle brought to life by the Master. The Doctor scares it off by holding out a piece of iron and muttering what seems to be a magical incantation. The iron is an old magical defence against such attacks, as he explains to Jo. She's puzzled why this worked on the gargoyle, because the Doctor doesn't believe in magic. He replies: 'I don't, but he does.' (A similar moment, of belief fending off evil, occurs in *The Curse of Fenric*, when one of the Russian soldiers fends off the Haemovores by the power of his faith, in this case, his faith in Soviet communism.)

Returning to the village, the Doctor arranges a little lecture, showing Jo, Miss Hawthorne and the UNIT soldiers a series of slides of deities from old religions. All the creatures he shows them have horns. His argument is that myths across the world share this one feature because they are based on something real: horned aliens who came to Earth in its prehistory. These aliens, Dæmons, helped to shape human development at various stages, and so 'all the magical traditions are just remnants of their advanced science'.

(Not cited, but impossible to ignore at this point, is 'Clarke's Law', a famous saying coined by the science fiction writer Arthur C Clarke: 'Any sufficiently advanced technology is indistinguishable from magic.' Clarke also posited, in his novel *Childhood's End* [1953] the idea of aliens who have overseen human history looking like the Devil, just as Azal does.)

While the Dæmons helped steer human development at certain points (the Renaissance, for instance), they were also perfectly happy to destroy civilisations that did not measure up to their standards. This was what happened to the lost civilisation of Atlantis. One of these aliens appears to be what caused the disaster at the Devil's Hump. The Master is trying to summon it and use it for his own ends. At the end of the story's third episode, there's a most unusual cliffhanger. The Master has summoned the Dæmon for what Miss Hawthorne suspects is the second of three occasions, but the ritual somehow goes wrong, and the Master himself is left cowering on the floor as the credits roll.

The story's final two episodes are mostly devoted to build-up before the Dæmon's climactic appearance. It's interesting how much of what follows is couched in the magical mode rather than the scientific. The Dæmon's speech patterns are very formal, and steer away from alluding to its scientific or technical knowledge. (At the same time as it's talking to the Master for the first time, the Doctor is trying to instruct a UNIT soldier on how to make a device work properly by reversing the polarity of the current flowing through a transistor. The contrast could not be starker.) The creature is eventually defeated by one of the show's less creditable pieces of plot-bodging. The Doctor's companion, Jo, offers her life to save the Doctor. Azal is so confused by this that he finds it impossible to bear, and destroys himself. To which one can only reply that if Azal and his race had observed the whole of history, this can hardly be the only piece of human irrationality they'd ever seen.

The Dæmons is so successful as a story, though, because it mostly recognises that the mythical mode is more fun to tell stories with. Many of its scenes would fit into more adult horror movies, and it certainly fulfils the role of *Doctor Who* to provide agreeable scariness for its audience. But there's no doubt that the Doctor's worldview is thoroughly borne out by the story. Every myth described in it is found to be in some way explicable, even if that explanation doesn't always make sense. An irrational atmosphere, like an atmosphere of fear, can be compounded out of rational things, a job which *The Dæmons* does superbly well.

THE SYCORAX (2005)

I n the *Doctor Who Magazine* preview for *The Christmas Invasion* (2005), to date the only story to feature the Sycorax, Russell T Davies says the following about them:

> I don't want to give too much away but in terms of design – not just their faces, but their clothes, their ship, their culture – we wanted to move away from militaristic, high-tech monsters. There's something spookier about the Sycorax. While I don't think magic exists in the Doctor Who universe, the 'magical' certainly does, and there's a slight supernatural feel to the Sycorax tribe. It really does feel like a great and terrible darkness is descending on the Earth...(Cook, 2005b, 23)

That distinction, between magic and the magical, is a very interesting one, and it'd be surprising if Davies. as thoroughgoing a *Doctor Who* fan as has lived, was not thinking of *The Dæmons* as he made it. The 'magical' is, after all, just a matter of seeming, and like *Aliens of London* one of the things *The Christmas Invasion* is about is not trusting first appearances.

It's a post-regeneration story. In the preceding episode, *The Parting of the Ways*, the Ninth Doctor (Christopher Eccleston) changes into the Tenth (David Tennant). At the start of *The Christmas Invasion*, the TARDIS lands glancingly at the home of the Doctor's companion, Rose, in contemporary London. For a good two-thirds of the hour-long episode, the Doctor remains comatose in a kind of post-regeneration shock. For that time, Rose is effectively the story's protagonist. She and her boyfriend, Mickey, go Christmas shopping, but they're attacked by robot Santa Clauses carrying trombones that double as projectile weapons. Back at home, their Christmas tree turns into a kind of pine-scented rotary saw and tries to kill them. The Doctor revives momentarily to neutralise the tree, but then slips back into his coma.

Up to this point, the effect of these set pieces is a little strange and estranging. A couple of Christmas icons have been made threatening and otherworldly, but nothing more than that. In another *Doctor Who* story, it might be expected that these would be knitted into the main plot, but all the explanation that's given is the Doctor's suggestion that the Santas and the tree are 'pilot fish', tiny scavengers that swim in advance of a far bigger threat. The bigger threat slowly becomes apparent. A UK space probe is destroyed on contact with a vast alien spaceship approaching Earth. Signals are received from red-robed aliens with skull-like helmets. The Prime Minister (Harriet Jones, a returning character from *Aliens of London*) attempts to deal with the crisis, but the skull-like aliens' language is difficult to understand. As the translation is slowly unpacked, the aliens' meaning becomes clear. They are called the Sycorax and they state, 'We own you. We now possess your land, your minerals, your precious stones, your women. You will surrender or they will die.' Harriet Jones sends a defiant reply back, and in response the Sycorax onscreen makes a strange gesture. (One of her aides says it's 'Almost like someone casting a spell.') It seems to have a hypnotic effect on a third of the world's population. They walk out of whatever room they are in, outdoors, and then up onto the roof of whatever tall building is nearest. There they stand together on the edge of the roof, as if waiting to jump.

Jones' team soon figures out that those affected by this hypnosis all share the same blood-group, A+, but this knowledge is of little help.

The next development is the arrival of the Sycorax ship over London, shattering windows and terrifying the populace. It's vast, and seemingly carved entirely from rock. Rose decides to get Mickey and the Doctor into the TARDIS along with provisions to sit out the crisis (tea, fruit and so on). But they soon find themselves transported up to the belly of the Sycorax ship along with Harriet Jones and some of her staff. There, the skull-like visage of the Sycorax is revealed to be a helmet, hiding their real face, all bone and flayed-seeming flesh. Their leader threatens Harriet Jones with 'the final curse' – magical language again – that he can force her people to jump. Rose attempts to bluff him with 'stolen words' picked up in her travels, but her attempt is transparent. Meanwhile, back in the TARDIS, the smell of tea revives the Doctor and he emerges from the TARDIS, now fully revived, to confront the Sycorax. Almost the first thing he does is to debunk their hold of the humans below. It's not magic, he says, but 'blood control', evidently a common technology that he finds easy to neutralise. (He explains that it's a trick like stage hypnosis. Although it can make people climb onto the roof, it could not make them go so strongly against their survival instincts as to jump.) So magic is not just explained as science, it's *superseded* by science.

The Doctor then challenges the Sycorax leader to a duel. The resulting swordfight (another deliberately archaic touch) leads them out onto the rocky surface of the ship. There, the Doctor falters, and his right hand is cut off. But, because he's within a few hours of his regeneration, he has enough energy left to regrow it. 'Witchcraft,' says the Sycorax leader. 'Time Lord,' replies the Doctor. Again, this is a broad hint that the Sycorax are limited because they can only think in quasi-magical terms. The Doctor fights back, defeats the Sycorax leader and orders his people to leave the planet.

Described in those terms, *The Christmas Invasion* sounds like a relatively straightforward story, in that sense, a suitable one for broadcast on Christmas Day. The presentation of the Sycorax certainly doesn't involve much moral ambiguity. Their desire to conquer Earth is almost unexplained, and very easy to parse as simply 'evil'. Nor is there any sense that any individual members of the Sycorax race might have any other shades of opinion from that embodied by their leader. So, in that sense, they are just monsters-who-are-there-to-be-monstrous. They're certainly well-designed, and presented in one of the new series' best-directed episodes. But I think they're elevated above the norm of *Doctor Who* monsters by what, in other circumstances, might be a flaw.

One criticism that's been made of Russell T Davies' writing is that, while he's very good at creating big set pieces (whether visual, emotional or both), he's not so good at the connective tissue between them, at giving those set pieces a context that allows them to make sense (see Chapter 10 on the Slitheen, and Bradshaw et al. 2011). *The Christmas Invasion* is certainly vulnerable to that criticism. As I've suggested, the set pieces with the musical Santas and the Christmas tree have hardly anything to do with the real plot, and the 'blood control' set piece of people standing hypnotised on their roofs also turns out to be fairly unimportant. But what they are, if nothing else, are fine pieces of atmosphere-building. (The first two are also shot at night, which helps.) These days, television series of all kinds seem to be composed more and more of trailers for themselves, short segments that 'throw forward' as the jargon has it and tell you what you'll see if you carry on watching. One of the most distinctive things about Davies' writing is how much he's integrated this idea into the fabric of his stories. *Doctor Who* has always, like much science fiction and fantasy, had a fondness for prophecies and the like. Davies has taken the trend to new extremes, as my summary of *The Christmas Invasion* should show. And prophecies do also have the feel of something magical and primitive – so beyond rational explanation. In the case of *The Christmas Invasion*, the rational explanation about 'pilot fish' isn't half as interesting as the spectacle it's supposed to explain. Many aspects of the Sycorax's design and performance dovetail with this: their jewellery, their primitive chanting, even their atavistic fear of the Doctor once he has defeated their leader. Even their name has magical overtones, being the name of the witch overthrown by Prospero in Shakespeare's *The Tempest*.

So *The Christmas Invasion* seems to me a very conscious effort to go down the same path as *The Dæmons* as much as *Doctor Who* can. It partakes of the glamour and strangeness of magic without ever suggesting that this might be a comprehensive explanation for the universe in the same way that science is. One of the important things about stage magic at least is knowing when not to explain things, and Davies does the same with the Sycorax. It actually helps the story that we're told so little about their origins and motivation. Magic depends on belief, and too many questions harm belief. Because the story doesn't ask those questions, it's easy to believe – as Davies said – that the Sycorax are somehow magical.

THE CYBERMEN II (1982–88)

The end of the first part of *Earthshock* (1982) is, for some, one of the great cliffhangers of *Doctor Who*'s history. The episode has followed an expedition in the twenty-sixth century to map the dinosaur fossils in a previously uncatalogued network of caves. The palaeontologists carrying out this work have started disappearing mysteriously, and so the military have been called in. Into this fraught situation comes the TARDIS, materialising in the caves. The Doctor and his companions are initially suspected by the military of being behind the deaths, but soon both they and the soldiers find themselves under attack from a pair of impassive black androids. A few shots are used of the androids' red-tinted point of view. As one such shot zeros in on the Doctor's face, there's a cut to the same image of his face, being viewed on some kind of scanner by two Cybermen. The Cyberleader instructs the androids, 'Destroy them. Destroy them at once!'

The effect of the ending is mostly derived from its shock value. The return of the Cybermen had not been trailed in any way, and so came as a total surprise to those watching at the time. Although they had been very effectively redesigned, the essential features of the creatures had not changed. It was, therefore, an ending that relied for its effect on knowing who the Cybermen were, and of being able to recognise them from a few seconds of image. Given that the Cybermen had not appeared on *Doctor Who* for seven years, this in turn meant that the viewers most rewarded by the ending were those who had a more than casual acquaintance with it.

Grouping together in one chapter the four Cyberman stories *Earthshock*, *The Five Doctors* (1983), *Attack of the Cybermen* (1985) and *Silver Nemesis* (1988) is more than just a matter of chronological convenience. I want to argue that these stories, often thrilling as they were to watch at the time, marked a turning-point for the worse in the series' history. The first cliffhanger of *Earthshock* is a signpost to the problem: a reliance on the series' history to an extent, and in a way, that made fans more important than nonfans. Later in the story, the Cybermen look back on their scanner to previous adventures in which they encountered the Doctor, a nod very much aimed at the series' past.

These Cybermen do seem more prone to emotion than their predecessors. They are certainly, at various points, angry, vengeful and even seem sadistic. (The story acknowledges this, with the Doctor noting that in comparison with some Cybermen he has met, the Cyberleader is 'positively flippant'.) Yet, as in earlier stories, the central debate in *Earthshock* is about what is lost in the conversion to Cyber-form. This is encapsulated in a conversation between the Doctor and the Cyberleader:

> **THE DOCTOR:** Emotions have their uses.
> **CYBERLEADER:** They restrict and curtail the intellect and logic of the mind.
> **THE DOCTOR:** They also enhance life! When did you last have the pleasure of smelling a flower, watching a sunset, eating a well-prepared meal?
> **CYBERLEADER:** These things are irrelevant.
> **THE DOCTOR:** For some people, small, beautiful events is what life is all about!

Despite a certain amount of bathos in that exchange ('eating a well-prepared meal'), it does stake out how different the Cybermen have made themselves from their original form. *Earthshock* is, if nothing else, a triumph of direction. Dimly lit caves, or the bowels of a spaceship, have never been made so spooky in *Doctor Who*. Nor have a small complement of Cybermen ever looked more like an army. The story's other great shock is reserved for its ending, when the Doctor's companion, Adric, is killed trying to save Earth. It was the first time a companion had died since *The Daleks' Masterplan* more than 15 years before. But the story doesn't really add to the mythos of the Cybermen. Indeed, it diminishes it. By giving them emotions, by allowing them to seem similar to humans, it robs them of what was most distinctive about them in the Troughton era.

The Cybermen returned in the 20th anniversary story, *The Five Doctors*, though their presence there was really as cannon fodder rather than substantive enemies. Most of the story takes place in a long-quarantined area of Gallifrey known as the Death Zone, where the Time Lords used to imprison lesser species to fight for their amusement. The Cybermen are shown as being consistently bamboozled by the Death Zone's hazards. Though they're not the only feature of *The Five Doctors*, the story does embody the queasily voyeuristic idea that lots of footage of Cybermen being blown up was sufficient amusement for Time Lords, and for viewers.

The nadir of this approach, and of the over-reliance on continuity I mentioned earlier, is marked by *Attack of the Cybermen*. There has been some controversy about its authorship over the years. It was attributed on broadcast to 'Paula Moore', the name of a freelance writer and friend of Saward, then in his penultimate season as script editor. But in the documentary accompanying its DVD release, Saward is explicit: it was almost entirely written by him, with marginal input from Moore and the series' unofficial continuity advisor Ian Levine. It certainly has plenty of the tropes Saward was fond of, blood and gore, mercenaries who work for the controlling aliens and kinetic action. It also, seemingly through Levine's influence, is bogged down with continuity references to the point of incoherence. Cybermen are present on Earth in the 1980s, attempting to prevent the destruction of Mondas (in *The Tenth Planet*) a few years hence. But they are controlled from Telos, some years after the events of *The Tomb of the Cybermen*, by the Cyber Controller. In order to glue this rickety structure together, the Cybermen must be equipped with time travel, but that still doesn't help it make sense. It's perhaps the most incoherent, and certainly the most continuity-burdened, story ever broadcast in the show's original run. Nor does it add much to the mythos of the Cybermen, beyond showing in graphic detail what their human-Cyberman transformation programme might entail.

Silver Nemesis was promoted as the series' 25th anniversary story, but it has come in for a significant amount of criticism since. Much of this is centred on its use of a very similar plot device to *Remembrance of the Daleks*, two stories earlier. In both, the Doctor confronts an old enemy on Earth. In both, the enemy is seeking an ancient Gallifreyan weapon which the Doctor seems to have had some hand in creating. In both, the enemy is defeated when they think they have control of the weapon, only to find that the Doctor has turned it against them. In this case, the ancient weapon is a statue called the Nemesis, made out of a 'living metal' and used by the Doctor to destroy a hidden fleet of Cyber ships orbiting the Earth.

Silver Nemesis is complicated by the presence of more adversaries than the Cybermen, who arrive at the end of the story's first episode (out of three). There is also a group of Nazis-in-hiding, who travel from their South American redoubt to capture the Nemesis statue. For all that they try to co-opt the Cybermen into their own mythos, seeing them as 'the Giants' in Wagnerian terms, the story, like its predecessor, fails to capitalise on the horror at the heart of these monsters. There is also a woman named Lady Peinforte, who travels from her home in the England of 1688 to the present day via in improvised 'magical' time travel. She knows something of the Nemesis statue, and believes she can use it to her advantage.

With all these plot-threads to be resolved in just 75 minutes of television, it's not surprising that things get more than a little confused. *Silver Nemesis* is certainly not as well directed or written a story as *Remembrance of the Daleks*. Nor does it do much to add to the mythos about its monsters as *Remembrance* does. But, partly because it's shot entirely on location, it does have a scope and range of settings that not many other *Doctor Who* stories do in this period. It shares, though, with the other stories discussed in this chapter, the same conception of the Cybermen, that they are as capable of pride or anger as the humans they oppose.

Perhaps the fault here lies not with the writers but with an actor. David Banks, a veteran of *Brookside*, played the Cyberleader in each of these stories. His is certainly the most memorable performance as a Cyberman in the series' history: He is implacable, ruthless and formidable. But the mere fact that it's a performance of that kind is a kind of problem. The Banks Cyberleader is always recognisable from his voice and gestures. There's no suggestion that his individuality had been submerged by the Cyber-conversion process. Personality, after all, is the opposite of what Cybermen should have.

THE MARSHMEN (1980)

A relatively common trope in written SF, though less frequent on television, is the idea that aliens encountered on some faraway planet have a peculiar life-cycle. Blundering human explorers may misinterpret what's going on, but more careful ones may arrive at a fuller understanding. (See, for instance, Orson Scott Card's *Speaker for the Dead* or James Tiptree Jr's *The Color of Neanderthal Eyes*.) Such a cerebral idea may be difficult to translate to television, but *Full Circle* (1980) is a distinguished attempt to do so. It falls in Tom Baker's last season as the Doctor, and is the first of three stories known informally as the 'E-Space trilogy'.

The story begins with the Doctor and his companion, Romana, in the TARDIS, where the Doctor has received a summons to return to their home planet Gallifrey. But something strange happens to the TARDIS in flight, and they materialise instead on a forest planet, Alzarius. There, the natives live a low-tech life, revolving around the plentiful sources of water, from which they gather 'riverfruit'. The story particularly follows a group of young 'Outlers', teenage rebels among whose number is Adric, soon to become one of the Doctor's companions. The Alzarian civilisation is governed from an immobile spaceship, the Starliner, where three 'Deciders' live, with access to their society's records and histories. These Deciders are monitoring various signs, such as the composition of the riverfruit, for hints of an approaching event called Mistfall. This only takes place once every few decades, but is clearly something they fear greatly. Throughout the story's first episode, there are signs that this is indeed about to happen. Wisps of fog billow in from the edge of shot, the water bubbles with smoke. On the strength of this, a Decider orders the riverside population to the safety of the Starliner. Then, at the end of the episodes, the river waters begin to boil and hideous creatures begin to rise from the swamp.

The emergence of these creatures, the Marshmen, is one of the best-executed cliffhangers in the series' history, beautifully framed and lit, and heightened with judicious use of slow motion. Of course, the appearance of some kind of swamp creature is a cliché of many SF films, not all of them good. But what makes *Full Circle* distinctive is the explanation that emerges over the next three episodes as to what these Marshmen are. There is no question that the Alzarians' fear is justified. The Marshmen are destructive, murderous and impossible to reason with. But that's not all they are. In appearance, they are humanoid, but with vaguely amphibian features. The sound effects accompanying their presence were the treated snortings of a group of pigs, a helpful shorthand for their animal nature. They're not, however, unintelligent, as they are repeatedly shown picking up pieces of wood or stone to use as weapons.

One unusual feature of the story is how little it requires the Doctor and Romana to do. They deduce fairly quickly that the anomaly the TARDIS passed through at the start of the story took them into 'E-Space', a pocket universe which appears to have what they thought was impossible, negative spatial coordinates. But the rest of the story is devoted to the bigger question of how Alzarius's society got to be the way it is. The story propagated by the Deciders is that the Starliner originated from a planet called Terradon. Damaged in flight, the Starliner landed on Alzarius many years before. The task before them, therefore, is to maintain and repair the

Starliner so that it can return them to Terradon. But there are a number of signs that this may not be the whole truth. The first is the dying words of one of the Deciders in the opening episode: 'We've come full circle.' The second is the presence of another life form in the ecosystem of Alzarius. These are spiders, introduced towards the end of the second episode as residents of a cave where the Outlers are hiding along with the TARDIS. Romana rather foolishly says that 'they're only spiders', is promptly bitten by one, and rapidly falls ill, with green-blue veins appearing on her face and neck. Meanwhile, the Doctor is at the Starliner, where he observes a scientist's examination of a young member of the Marshmen's species. Enraged by the scientist's cavalier attitude to the ethics of what he's doing, the Doctor instead confronts the Deciders with the true state of affairs. The Starliner has been ready to take off 'for centuries'. The Deciders, however, have created needless work to obscure this fact, but as their leader confesses, no one knows how to pilot the ship.

Meanwhile, Romana, her mind affected by the spiders' venom, opens the ground-level hatches on the Starliner so that vast numbers of Marshmen can enter. Despite the chaos this causes, the Doctor makes his way to the Starliner's laboratory and completes his investigations. He finds an antidote for Romana's infection, and then begins looking at tissue samples from the three species central to the story: Marshmen, spiders and humans. He deduces that they are all different forms of the same species. The humans now inhabiting the Starliner are not the original travellers from Terradon, who were presumably killed by the Marshmen years before, but instead genetic cousins of the Marshmen. Hence the lack of knowledge about how to pilot the Starliner, and the Deciders' corrosive secrecy about their society's history. Despite all this, and the knowledge that the 'humans' in the story are indeed Alzarians, they decide that they do wish to fly the Starliner away from Alzarius. They cannot return to Terradon, but may instead find another new home. As the Doctor says, late in the story, the Marshmen are not 'horrible'. 'We're all basically just primeval slime with ideas above its station.' He gives the Deciders the knowledge they need to fly the ship, and then departs in the TARDIS, seeking a way out of E-Space.

So *Full Circle* is a story that takes as a given the idea of evolution: the idea that environmental pressures can transform one form of life, over time, into another. It's also very much concerned with the idea of what is and isn't 'primitive'. The Marshmen may look, act and be shot as if they're generic *Doctor Who* monsters, there (like Kroll) to rise from the swamp and cause havoc whenever the story requires it. And there's certainly no question that they can be communicated with or have their nature changed. But the point of the story is that the supposedly civilised humans are much closer to the Marshmen than they might like to think. Indeed, the humans have created vast structures of deception and denial to try to avoid this possibility ever being seen as the truth. This process of denial has been so effective that it's come to be accepted as the unquestioned reality. As on a few occasions in the series' history, detailed scientific investigation is at the heart of the story, overturning this myth. It also overturns, as I suggested earlier, the idea of a clean divide between the 'civilised' humans and the 'primitive' Marshmen. The last scenes of the story, once this knowledge is out in the open, provide some truly eerie moments. We've earlier seen the Marshmen rampaging round the Starliner, and it's clear that they don't belong there. But at the end of the story, we know that the humans don't belong there either. Its corridors and chambers are no more theirs than the Marshmen's. At the heart of the story is an absence that can never be filled: the unseen original travellers from Terradon, whose fate remains a mystery, and whose bones are presumably lying somewhere in the swamps. Although the Doctor, and the scientific method he uses, can reveal the truth of what's going on, he can't unmake it.

THE OOD
(2006, 2008, 2009–10, 2011)

I n their appearances to date, the Ood have seemed radically different creatures. Although their appearance has not
changed, they have always been humanoid creatures with
grey tentacled heads, what they do in stories has changed.
One passing reference in their second story suggests they're
related to the Sensorites, creatures introduced in a 1964
William Hartnell story. But the Ood are depicted with much
greater sophistication.

In *The Impossible Planet/The Satan Pit* (2006), the Doctor
and Rose land on a planet in a stable orbit around a black
hole. Despite this being, as the title says, impossible, there is
a human-staffed scientific research base there, observing and
attempting to work out what's happening. The human staff
is supplemented by a crew of Ood, who seem to be obedient
servants. Their manner may be a little disconcerting, as may
be the strange spheres they carry, which light up when they
speak. But they are hardly an obvious threat. The Doctor is
instead preoccupied by a number of inexplicable inscriptions
around the base, which slowly lead him to the conclusion that

there is something very strange buried beneath the surface. When he finally reaches this at the end of the second episode, it turns out to be nothing less than the devil, or, at least, a huge creature that looks very like the Judeo-Christian idea of the devil. Before he has arrived there, though, this creature has at various times possessed the Ood, making them attack the humans and announce the return of 'the Beast'. In this story, in other words, the Ood are not centre stage. At the end, the Doctor notes with some sadness that he was only able to save the humans, not the Ood, from the calamity that destroys the devil-creature. This is as direct an acknowledgment as the story makes that the Ood are sentient like the humans, and should be treated as such.

Planet of the Ood (2008) is a very different tale. It takes place on Ood-Sphere, the creatures' frigid home. The planet is adorned with a human-built factory in which the Ood are processed so that they can be sold as servants, or, more exactly, slaves. The very first scene depicts a human executive in this company, 'Ood Operations', mulling a price cut for the creatures, only to be murdered by the Ood supposed to be serving him. This creature is affected with glowing red eyes. Soon after, a man named Halpen, the chief executive of the company exploiting the Ood, lands. He is told that there have been several such incidents; the Ood appear to kill their victims by putting the spheres they carry, the 'translator-balls', to the victims' heads. He is also told of 'red-eye', which is thought to be some kind of infection carried by the creatures, and which seems to be correlated with their violent behaviour. So, from the start, the Ood are treated by the humans as *property*, as creatures with no agency or sentience worth considering, and whose enslavement is morally neutral. (And, since they sell in their millions, it can be assumed this attitude is shared widely outside the company.)

Meanwhile, the Doctor lands outside the factory complex with his new companion, Donna. They find an Ood dying in the snow. Donna is shocked by 'its face', but the Doctor quickly corrects her: 'It's a he, not an it.' The Ood's translator-ball still works, and he tells the Doctor that his designation is Ood Delta-50. He has been shot, and seems to be the same creature who committed the murder in the episode's opening scene. He then gives the cryptic message that 'the circle must be broken', rears up with a roar and a flash of red eyes, and then slumps back dead. The Doctor and Donna inveigle their way into the factory complex for a tour. During this, the company's marketing staff portray the Ood as 'happy to serve', kept in conditions of good quality and 'healthy, safe and educated'. In other words, their slavery is rationalised in various ways: Humans are actually doing the Ood a favour (the pretext runs), helping them to achieve as much as possible given their nature. In a reception run by the company, Donna pushes this point by asking one of the creatures whether there are any Ood who are 'wild', outside this system. The Ood tells her that 'All Ood are born to serve', but further questioning seems to disconcert the creature, and it begins talking about 'the circle', just like the one in the snow.

Halpen and his colleagues are trying to deal with the epidemic of red-eye and the ensuing violence. As they ponder its causes, Halpen goes to Warehouse 15 on the factory site, where something vast and secret is hidden. What's there isn't revealed at this point, but it clearly disgusts and intrigues Halpen. At the same time, the Doctor and Donna are discovering the scope of the Ood-as-slaves operation. They discover a vast warehouse filled with cargo containers, each packed with seemingly docile Ood. There is some pointed dialogue as they absorb the consequences of this:

> **DONNA:** A great big empire built on slavery.
> **THE DOCTOR:** It's not so different from your time.
> **DONNA:** Oi, I haven't got slaves!
> **THE DOCTOR:** Who do you think made your clothes?
> **DONNA:** Is that why you travel round with a human at your side? It's not so you can show them the wonders of the universe, it's so you can take cheap shots.
> **THE DOCTOR:** Sorry.

These Ood too repeat the mantra that 'the circle must be broken', adding 'so that we can sing.' But any further investigation is impossible as the Doctor and Donna are pursued by the company's security forces. They find their way to another building, called 'Ood conversion', where the creatures are caged but in their natural state. Instead of the artificial translator-spheres, they instead carry 'a secondary brain' on a long translucent cord emerging from their mouths. The Doctor explains: 'Like the amygdala in humans, it processes memory and emotions.' The company removes these organs and replaces them with the translator-spheres.

With this butchering of the Ood now clear, and also the telepathic 'song' they can exude in their natural state, the Doctor and Donna are captured and taken to Halpen. He proposes to gas the rogue Ood in the container warehouse, 'the classic foot-and-mouth solution from the olden days...still works.' But it doesn't; the Ood instead use their telepathy to spread the red-eye contagion throughout the complex. Halpen's assistant, Ood Sigma, seems to be the last one free of red-eye. The Doctor deduces that there must be some kind of Ood creature that they have yet to see and, in the chaos resulting from the red-eye 'revolution', he and Donna follow Halpen to Warehouse 15. Halpen is planning to destroy what is kept there, a vast central brain for the whole Ood species, and the nexus of their telepathy. It's surrounded by a ring of electrical pylons which contains it and damps down the creatures' telepathic field, no doubt, the circle that the Ood want to be broken. But Halpen begins feeling unwell, and begins to suspect that Ood Sigma has been poisoning him. Instead of the hair tonic he has been persistently asking for through the episode, he has been fed 'Ood graft suspended in a biological compound'. His proximity to the Ood brain finally activates its effects, transforming him into an Ood. There's an obvious irony here, since the Ood were what he most despised and feared. The Doctor deactivates the pylons around the Ood brain, the telepathic field is reactivated again and the Ood on this world and many others are set free. As the Doctor and Donna are leaving, though, Ood Sigma tells them, 'I think your song must end soon.'

This prophecy is revisited two years later, in the Tenth Doctor's final stories, *The Waters of Mars* (2009) and *The End of Time* (2009–10). In the first, the Doctor does what he knows he should not, and saves a group of colonists on Mars from the death that he knows they suffer in history. Taking them back to Earth, he confronts their leader, Adelaide Brooke, who has come to realise that her survival, and the Doctor's intervention, were somehow against the natural order of things. She goes into her house alone, and the Doctor hears a single shot as she kills herself. He turns round to see Ood Sigma standing silently in the snow, and recognises that this signals his impending death. (There was, in any case, some forewarning of this in the previous story, *Planet of the Dead* [2009].) But the Ood fades away without saying anything.

At the start of *The End of Time*, the Doctor brings the TARDIS to Ood-Sphere, where he is again met by Ood Sigma. The Ood tells him that 'You should not have delayed', as the Doctor says, he spent a great deal of time travelling before coming to what he knew might be his death. He is taken to a group of Ood elders who, using their telepathy, share the visions they have. As I suggested in the chapter on the Sycorax, prophecies and foreshadowings act, especially in Davies' *Doctor Who*, as trailers for the rest of the episode. That's certainly the case here, as we're shown in short order the main antagonist, the Master, and a number of other characters.

The Ood don't appear in the bulk of the story, but there's a sense in which their telepathy and prophecy frame it, so, once the Doctor has defeated the Master's plan, there's a further shot of them signalling that all is well. Telepathy gives them a kind of perfect benign honesty. So, when Tennant's Doctor is dying, Ood Sigma again appears to him to 'sing [him] to [his] sleep'.

Throughout the Ood's first three appearances, certain characteristics of monsters are used to the stories' advantage. Because they lack the kind of facial expressions that we can read, they appear inscrutable, and their placid, even voices convey the same message. Their occasional leaps into red-eyed rage are therefore all the more shocking. In the last two stories, they're also shown to have a culture strongly based around music. This gives them both a depth they might not otherwise have and it also allows them to have a presence in the show's soundtrack (as, for instance, in Tennant's last moments.) In the post-2005 series, the Time Lords have gone from the universe, and so has their role as arbiter of what's permissible in the universe. Indeed, Tennant's last three episodes are in various ways a discussion of the consequences of this. The Ood take on some of this function in these episodes, their presence indicating that the Doctor has gone too far. It's hard to think of another creature in the show that's made the same transition, from monsters-with-intent-to-frighten to the creators of an all but utopian society.

Sadly, the last appearance of an Ood, in Neil Gaiman's *The Doctor's Wife* (2011) is the least interesting thing about an otherwise extraordinary story. It's an episode that pulls inside-out the entire history of the series, showing its central relationship as that between the Doctor and the TARDIS, who is here incarnated in the body of a woman called Idris. The Ood is used as a by-the-numbers scary monster (replacing, apparently, a new monster originally created by Gaiman and then cut for cost reasons). But it's an interesting mark of the show's twenty-first-century evolution that a creature like the Ood can so quickly be taken as read.

THE THARILS (1981)

The Tharils and the Ood deserve to be considered together, because both are slave races whose apparent ferocity in fact derives from how they have been treated. The Tharils appear in *Warriors' Gate* (1981), the last story of the 'E-Space Trilogy' begun by *Full Circle*.

Before discussing the story, it's worth saying that *Warriors' Gate* had one of the most complex and troubled productions of any *Doctor Who* story. This background is discussed by many of the participants in 'The Dreaming', a fascinating documentary on the recent DVD release of the story. The credited author of *Warriors' Gate*, Stephen Gallagher, is now better known as one of the UK's most notable horror writers, and is very candid in admitting that his first draft of the story was closer to being a novel than a shootable script. The final version of the script was principally composed by Christopher H Bidmead, then the script editor, with input from Paul Joyce, the story's director. From his testimony in the documentary, it seems that Joyce responded very strongly to the script from the start, and despite his inexperience in television direction was hugely ambitious in what he tried to achieve in production. He rapidly got behind schedule, alienated the technical staff and was called in for a dressing-down by the executive producer. Joyce was briefly fired from the production, then reinstated, and the story needed a great deal of further tweaking in the post-production phase. All this was in the context of a story that, in any case, was one of the densest and most conceptually ambitious *Doctor Who* had ever attempted.

The story begins on a human-crewed 'Privateer' ship. The Privateer ship is steered by an imprisoned representative of the Tharil race. Others of these tall leonine creatures are kept under sedation in the hold. (Gallagher's original script specified that they were to look like the Beast from Cocteau's *La Belle et La Bête*.) The Tharils are the only creatures capable of navigating the 'Time winds' that flow around a gateway such as this. Atypically, and interestingly for *Doctor Who*, the crew are depicted as being lazy, apathetic and bored. Only Rorvik, the captain, seems to have enough energy to drive them anywhere. As the ship enters the rift that brought it the void, their Tharil navigator Biroc escapes, and he soon arrives at the TARDIS. He should not be able to enter the Doctor's ship, but does. While there, he appears to be 'out of phase', but manages to set the TARDIS's controls so that they are 'locked off at zero'. The ship has landed in a strange white void, which also now contains the Privateer ship and an incongruous, medieval-seeming stone gateway. Biroc makes his way to this structure, followed by the Doctor. Within is a dusty, disused banqueting hall, surrounded by mirrors. Biroc passes through one of these and vanishes. Instead of following him, the Doctor becomes interested by some seemingly motionless armoured knights. Two of these come to life, try to attack him, but end up knocking each other out. Investigating their forms, the Doctor confirms that they are robots, and he manages to get one of them to speak to him.

The speech that follows is quite extraordinary. Even though it occurs only in the second of the story's four episodes, it gives away much of the story's background. The robot identifies itself as one of a race called the Gundans, constructed to overthrow the tyrannical slave-holding regime ruled by

Biroc's race, the Tharils. So there's a degree of moral ambivalence introduced: the Tharils, once the owners of human slaves, are now themselves slaves of humans. Moreover, it's clear that the mirrors in the banqueting hall are the gateway out of E-Space that the Doctor has been seeking. The Doctor passes though one of the mirrors, and finds Biroc. Behind the mirrors is a strange realm, rendered as static monochrome photographs of the gardens of a stately home, thorough which the Doctor and Biroc move in colour. The effect is haunting, as if this world of Biroc's, even more than the banqueting hall, is frozen in aspic. The Doctor is led by a female Tharil through endless halls until he is brought to an arch overlooking the same banqueting hall he'd earlier left, but this time with the Tharils in their pomp, feasting. The banquet is interrupted as the Gundans enter, swinging their axes, and the Doctor finds himself back in the cobweb-covered hall, with Rorvik and his crew surrounding him. At gunpoint, he is gestured to one of the mirrors, and he speaks with Biroc on the other side of the glass:

> **THE DOCTOR:** Hello, Biroc.
>
> **BIROC:** Doctor. You've seen our past. You've seen our present. You were right. We abused our power. But judge whether we have not suffered enough.
>
> **THE DOCTOR:** As you said, the weak enslave themselves.
>
> **BIROC:** The time of our enslavement is over. We will be free.
>
> **THE DOCTOR:** I wish you luck. But what about us?

'What about us?' is an important question, because K-9 has just brought all concerned some disturbing news. The void in which the drama is taking place is contracting, and as space contracts, so does time. (Hence the rupture that brought the Doctor from one version of the banqueting hall to the other.) What's causing this is an excess of mass. Rorvik's ship is made from dwarf star alloy, the only material that can imprison the Tharils. Its huge density is causing the contraction. A stand-off occurs, and the Doctor and his companions retreat to the TARDIS. Rorvik formulates a plan. He will try to break his ship out of the void by a 'backblast' from its engines. While the power is building, the Doctor and Romana set off to set free the Tharils kept in Rorvik's hold. But the Tharils are in the end able to free themselves, and leave through the gateway and the mirrors. The TARDIS dematerialises (although Romana leaves, somewhat abruptly, taking K-9 to help Biroc and his people) and the Privateer ship's engines do, as predicted, destroy both it and the gateway.

What will be apparent from this is how much more sophisticated *Warriors' Gate* is in its treatment of slavery than *Planet of the Ood*. Here, the same species can be both slave and enslaver. Moreover, the portrait of the humans aboard the Privateer ship is far more realistic than that of those in *Planet of the Ood*. The Tharils are treated with a kind of casual indifference that rings far more true than the highly-charged almost-fear that the representatives of the Ood Corporation have. Putting it very crudely, in *Warriors' Gate*, it's much less clear who the audience should sympathise with, who the good guys are.

More than any other story I consider in this book, *Warriors' Gate* raises the question of who the audience for *Doctor Who* is. In 'The Dreaming', the documentary mentioned above, Lalla Ward (who played Romana) mentions it as exemplifying a move in the series away from pleasing children and towards an older audience. She was, it's clear, not at all happy with this move. The ratings for *Warrior's Gate* were low, but they were low for much of the rest of its season, principally because of how the show was scheduled, rather than any other cause. Eight- or ten-year-olds can hardly be expected to catch references to *La Belle et La Bête* or the I Ching, and even now, the full intricacies of the time travel story are a little opaque. The moral ambivalence of the Tharils, the surreal visual style and the oblique manner of telling, could all have put viewers off. *Warriors' Gate* is not the kind of experiment the show has returned to, nor have the Tharils ever reappeared. For once, though, it's a story in which the Doctor's sympathies are fully with the aliens rather than the humans. By giving them an appearance that evokes lions, the story evokes all the myths of pride and nobility associated with that species (as does

John Crowley's novel *Beasts* [1976], whose 'leos' have much in common with the Tharils). *Warriors' Gate* is part of a much larger story that's only partly spelt out here, but it's the part that sees the Tharils redeemed. That too is rare for a *Doctor Who* monster, and one of the things that makes the Tharils so memorable.

THE CYBERMEN III
(2006, 2008, 2011)

The revived series of *Doctor Who*, running from 2005 to date, has given four monsters from the 'classic' series substantive appearances. The Sontarans' return is discussed in Chapter 9, that of the Silurians in Chapter 11 and that of the Daleks in Chapter 32. The return of the Cybermen, in the 2006 story *Rise of the Cybermen/The Age of Steel*, is perhaps most emblematic of the way in which the new series revises and updates old concepts.

Given the complexity, or, frankly, chaos, of the timeline for the Cybermen in the classic series, the solution chosen by Russell T Davies and his fellow producers has a certain elegant simplicity. They dispensed with all past Cyberman continuity and set the new adventure in a parallel world where the creatures' development had taken an entirely different course. In an early scene of *Rise of the Cybermen*, the TARDIS slips through into an alternate world where the sky of contemporary London is filled with zeppelins. Crucially, the Doctor's companion, Rose, sees from an advertising billboard that (unlike in 'her' world) her father Pete is alive, well and advertising fizzy drinks. While she goes to look for him, the real plot is slowly becoming clear. This alternate world is dominated by the products of a company called Cybus Industries, run by a crippled genius called John Lumic. Lumic is terminally ill, and he has been secretly developing the Cybermen, ultimately to serve as a vehicle for his brain when his body fails. But he also uses the other devices produced by Cybus, such as mobile phones and Bluetooth-like earpieces, to exert a kind of mental control over those who carry them.

Lumic's Cybermen are initially created from the bodies of homeless people abducted by his staff. (This continues a theme of the new *Doctor Who* that the most vulnerable in society are most likely to fall victim to this kind of exploitation. In *The Parting of the Ways*, the Dalek Emperor says that his new Daleks have also been taken from the same group.) However, in *The Age of Steel*, with crisis now threatening, Lumic orders that all those wearing earpods in London be made to report for 'upgrading'.

This kind of language is one of the more interesting things about the story. Cybermen have always seen themselves as superior to humans, but here this argument is clothed in the terms contemporary business-speak. At other times, the Cybermen describe themselves as 'Human point 2', as if peoples' nature could be changed as easily as software versions. The use of mobile phones and earpieces as Lumic's tools fits with this idea. The Cyberman stories have always been technophobic, but mostly in the abstract. A child watching, say, *The Tomb of the Cybermen* could imagine the horror of being converted. But *Rise of the Cybermen* features the most graphic depiction yet of the process of being converted into a Cyberman. In the first episode, a group of Lumic's abductees are herded into a vast factory space filled with steel vats. We are shown each of them shuffling into one of these vats and then, from their viewpoint, the whirring and buzzing of savage-looking surgical implements as their brains are parted from their bodies.

These new Cybermen are, far more than those considered in Chapter 19, truly emotionless. Their voices (provided by Nicholas Briggs) are closer to the expressionless ones used in the Troughton era than the more nuanced ones that appeared in *Earthshock* and subsequent stories. They are rigidly doctrinaire in obeying orders, and emotion is anathema to them. In fact, this becomes the means of their defeat, just as in *The Invasion*. In the earlier story, Tobias Vaughan's secret card in his bargaining with the Cybermen is a device that exposes them to the emotions excised from their body and so kills them. Here, the Doctor finds the code that will disrupt the 'emotional inhibitor' mechanism, with the same effect.

Cyber-stories have always had an edge of satire to them, directed at humanity's increasing (and excessive?) reliance on technology. As we've seen earlier, in the 1960s, this was directed at transplant surgery and similar intrusions into the body. Four decades later, the choice of mobile technology seems far more apposite, even though Davies-era *Doctor Who* also often features mobile phones as a positive plot device (for Rose Tyler to speak to her mother, for instance). One of the emblematic sights of twenty-first-century life, at least in the UK, is of people walking down the street oblivious to their surroundings because they're having conversations with others who aren't there. The first episode of *Rise of the Cybermen* takes this a step further, with a fascinating set piece in an ordinary pedestrianised city street. The Doctor and Rose are the only people in this street without 'earpods', and so they look on in some shock when everyone else stops dead at the same time. They are, it becomes clear, receiving information over their earpods. (When a joke is delivered, everyone laughs at the same moment.) Then the information download is over, and people go back to their business. This is a moment that doesn't bear thinking about too much (what if someone's wearing an earpod while crossing the road, or driving a lorry?), but it makes the point effectively. Devices like these take us away from the world we're in. In that respect, they're the first step towards losing one's humanity and becoming Cybermen.

The Cybermen returned in the finale of the same season, in *Army of Ghosts/Doomsday* (2006). This story doesn't particularly augment the new conception of the Cybermen, but does give them some spectacular new set pieces. It's mainly set in 'our' world, where 'ghosts' have been appearing for some months. Aided by an organisation called the Torchwood Institute, their presence has been increasing, something that makes the Doctor profoundly worried. At the end of the first episode, it's made clear that the ghosts are surviving Cybermen from Lumic's world, who have been able to break through the barrier between worlds. A vast army of them finally materialises across the globe, ready to conquer. However, as part of the same cliffhanger, a spherical spaceship held for many years by Torchwood and resistant to analysis up to this point finally opens to reveal four Daleks. These are the Cult of Skaro (see Chapter 32).

This cliffhanger sets up a final-episode confrontation that many fans have waited years to see, Daleks vs. Cybermen. Despite being hugely outnumbered, it's clear that the Daleks are far superior to the Cybermen, unsurprisingly given how much more advanced their technology is. But the Cybermen go on converting the human staff of Torchwood, including its head, Yvonne Hartman. Yvonne does seem able to resist the conversion process, though, and the Cyberman created from her manages to fight back and resist its conditioning.

The overwhelming message, though, from these episodes, is that Cyber-conversion is total, radical and savage, and that it's a line of thinking that our current reliance on mobile technology may take us down. The Cybermen and Daleks are both eventually defeated by being exiled to the 'Void' between worlds, but in the meantime, they've provided some spectacular set pieces that would have been beyond the reach of the old series: a suburban street filled with Cybermen, for instance, a family home being taken over by them.

The Cybermen's final substantive appearance to date was in a Christmas special, *The Next Doctor* (2008). This story is set in Victorian London, where Lumic-era Cybermen have emerged from their exile in the Void. They have enlisted the help of a woman named Miss Hartigan, who runs a children's workhouse, because they need a labour force for their next project, creating a 'Cyberking'. The London streets are also haunted by creatures called Cybershades, which seem to be animal/Cybermen hybrids, though their origins are never fully explained.

The Cyberking is, and there's no other way to put it, a giant robot designed to stomp London into the ground. It makes sense that the Cybermen would be able to create a creature like this. Up to this point, we've never seen them with any means of transport or destruction, other than space-ships. If, as seems likely, the Cybermen need to fight battles, then it's not surprising that they need battlefield weapons of this kind.

The story has two very different emotional lines running through it. The first is the narrative of Jackson Lake, a teacher who came to London to take up a new job. His wife and children were killed by the Cybermen and this trauma, cou-pled with the absorption of information from a Cyber-created 'info-stamp', leads him to believe that he is the Doctor, the man whose history was recorded on the info-stamp. For the first half of the story, there is uncertainty as to whether he might in fact be a future incarnation of the Doctor. His final understanding of what has really happened to him is very moving, particularly thanks to David Morrissey's perform-ance as Lake. The second is the story of Miss Hartigan. It's clear that she's made a devil's bargain with the Cybermen, and in story terms is likely to receive her comeuppance.

This eventually comes about towards the end of the story, when the Cybermen force her into the control chair of the Cyberking and so 'convert' her. They have sensed the anger and hatred that has driven her (there's a hinted-at story here about how difficult it would be to be an intelligent and ambi-tious woman in this time and place). So they decide, to her fury, to free her from it. The final confrontation in the story is between the Doctor (travelling in a hot air balloon owned by Lake) and the Hartigan-steered balloon. Using an info-stamp, he breaks the connection between her and the Cyberking. As in *The Age of Steel*, the way to defeat these creatures is to return to them their emotions, and so show them what they have become.

The Cybermen also make a brief appearance in *Closing Time* (2011), where they are the alien threat underlying a story of the Doctor's visit to his old friend Craig Owens. They're really secondary, though, to the story of Craig's emotional shift as he becomes a truly loving father. This requires some shifts in the Cyberman mythos: the climax of the story is a Cyber-conversion performed on Craig that's reversed when he discovers the healing power of love. The objection here isn't particularly that Cyber-conversions haven't been reversible at any point in the series before then. The objection is that *Doctor Who* is, all too often in its twenty-first-century life, using the same plot device as its final pivot. Some very fine stories use the redemptive power of love as their final turn, for instance, *Father's Day* (2005) and *The Empty Child/The Doctor Dances* (2005). But so do some much less good ones. *Closing Time* is in fact one of the funniest and best-performed episodes of *Doctor Who* ever, but it diminishes the threat of the Cybermen and what they represent.

In *The Next Doctor* and *Closing Time* the Cybermen are a known threat, whose origins and rationale don't need to be reexamined. The Cybershades and the Cyberking are new additions to the mythos, but they're not explained except as new threats to the Doctor. But the new series' approach to these monsters is one of its most interesting features. It has examined what made them terrifying in the first place, thoughtfully updated this origin story and then provided a story that puts their strengths onscreen in as large a scale as possible.

THE ADIPOSE (2008)

The first episode of the revived *Doctor Who*'s fourth series, *Partners in Crime* (2008), stretched the format as far towards comedy as it's ever gone. The story is set on contemporary Earth, and its larger purpose is to enable the Doctor and Donna, who met before in the Christmas special *The Runaway Bride*, to be reunited and to travel together in the TARDIS.

The Adipose are the notional monsters of this episode, but they stretch the definition a long way. Although they are involved in the death of one character that we see, it's hardly their responsibility. The safe departure from Earth of multitudes of them at the end of the episode is hardly a sad occasion; the right thing has happened. But they do meet one basic criterion for being monsters: they scare people.

At the end of *The Runaway Bride*, the Doctor had offered Donna, the bolshy secretary who had helped him defeat an attempted invasion of Earth by the Racnoss, the chance to travel with him in the TARDIS. She declined, saying instead that she would travel the Earth instead, and 'walk in the dust'. At the start of *Partners in Crime*, it seems instead that she's become a kind of investigator into the kinds of phenomena that the Doctor is interested in. Specifically, she's looking into the activities of an organisation called Adipose Industries, which has recently begun offering a trouble-free weight-loss solution. All its users need to do is wear a special pendant, take some pills and 'the fat just walks away'.

The Doctor is also present at this time and place, and also investigating Adipose Industries. By a series of shots that verge on farce (deliberately, to judge by the DVD commentary) on farce, the Doctor and Donna keep missing each other as they try to track down what's really happening. The first specifics arrive as they each go to the house of a different user of the Adipose service. The man the Doctor meets claims he's lost exactly 14 kgs, 1 kg a day for the last fortnight. He knows this because each night he's awoken at 1.10 am by his burglar alarm going off. It seems that something might be getting out of his cat flap and triggering the motion sensors. The woman Donna meets, Stacey, tells a similar story. But something goes wrong. While Stacey is in the bathroom, Donna is tinkering with an Adipose pendant she's carrying, and this seems to cause strange side effects. Stacey hears her stomach growling, and something seems to be trying to break out under her skin. (In the Adipose Industries headquarters, we also hear a warning message flagging 'unscheduled parthenogenesis'.) Finally a creature pops out (without blood or trauma, and seemingly without causing pain). It's perhaps nine inches high, white and has little arms and feet and a face that can only be described as 'cute'.

By this point, the viewer will have picked up the hint that this is an Adipose, the name coming, it's safe to say, from the adipose tissue which constitutes human body fat. They will further have guessed that the emergence of these Adipose is being engineered by Adipose Industries through their pills and pendants. Meanwhile, though, Donna can only listen from the other side of the bathroom door as Stacey disintegrates into her component Adipose, leaving only a pile of clothes behind.

Soon enough, the Doctor and Donna find themselves at the headquarters of Adipose Industries, where they are putting together more pieces of the puzzle, though still separately. Miss Foster, the woman running the company, has an immediate problem to deal with, an investigative journalist digging into how its technology works. With the journalist safely restrained by her security team, Miss Foster begins to explain the process. The pills, she explains, bind the fat together and galvanises it to form a body. She is a kind of 'foster mother' to the Adipose, whom she is here on Earth to breed safely from human fat. In a further conversation with the Doctor, she explains that she is using humans as surrogates, having been employed by the Adiposian first family to create a new generation of the creatures after their breeding planet was lost.

This confrontation ends in a stand-off, and Miss Foster instead triggers off 'premature labour'. Vast numbers of Adipose start leaving their human hosts. This produces the memorable image of whole streets overwhelmed with Adipose, like drifts of snow ambling along. They finally congregate around the Adipose Industries building, and a vast spaceship arrives overhead to collect them. The Adipose gently waft up into the blinding light it sheds (again, like film of snow, run backwards) but, as the Doctor warns, Miss Foster is killed, her usefulness exhausted.

On one level, the Adipose Industries set up is the same kind of story I've described in earlier chapters about the Primords and the Axons. Any scientific advance that looks too good to be true probably is, and so viewers should be cautious about them. This is *Doctor Who* in the realm of cautionary tales. But that doesn't quite explain the form or the behaviour of the monsters. In his DVD commentary on the episode, Russell T Davies describes how, in writing it, he could have given the Adipose snapping jaws or similar monster-like attributes, but decided not to, partly because it had been done before, and partly because he wanted this episode to be broadly comic in tone. But there is, I think, another reason.

The initial visuals of Stacey's stomach stretching as the Adipose try to break out are very reminiscent of the famous, and gory, 'chest-burster' sequence in Ridley Scott's *Alien*. Such a scene would be unthinkable in *Doctor Who*, of course, because of the family audience it tries to attract. Moreover, unlike Scott's alien, the Adipose are not something foreign to the bodies they emerge from. Rather, they're a part of it, grown over years as part of its tissue. And it's difficult to think of a part of one's own body, certainly a part like a slightly oversized stomach, as malicious or evil. So the Adipose are gently benign because to make them otherwise would introduce ideas that this story probably can't accommodate about, say, people feeling uncomfortable in or hating their bodies.

I'm arguing throughout this book that monsters represent individual bits of human nature. In the case of the Adipose, it's almost too easy to say what that individual bit is, the excess weight that many people (including this author) would like to get rid of. The Adipose story has a great deal in common with the rebirth of the Cybermen under John Lumic, as described in the last chapter. It's not just that a too-easy solution has been provided by technology, it's that that solution has been bundled up and *packaged* by a corporate entity. There's a sense that many people are following the Adipose treatment for the same reason they follow diet fads, because of social pressure, because it's the fashionable thing to do.

So in this case, the monster represents a solution to a problem that many people have. What makes it monstrous, or at least something that the Doctor needs to stop, is that the solution is too easy. It's almost impossible to find the Adipose anything but cute, there's no *Doctor Who* monster more suitable for making into a cuddly toy. Science fiction tends to take abstract ideas and make them literal, as with many other monsters in this book. The point of the Adipose is that literalising fat is bad for you.

THE ICE WARRIORS
(1967, 1969, 1972, 1973)

Although they have not appeared in the series for more than 35 years, the Ice Warriors are one of the most fondly remembered of *Doctor Who* monsters. Their first appearance, in *The Ice Warriors*+ (1967) is pretty clearly their strongest, even though two of the story's six episodes are missing from the archives. Their subsequent stories, *The Seeds of Death* (1969), *The Curse of Peladon* (1972) and *The Monster of Peladon* (1973), are perfectly adequate pieces of *Doctor Who*, but not on the same level.

The premise of *The Ice Warriors* is a near-future Britain where climate change has caused a new Ice Age. (In fact, the story suggests that this might be caused by mass deforestation, exactly the opposite of current climate change fears. But that's a minor point.) At various points around the globe, the glaciers are held back by ionisers, devices best understood as heat generators. The story is set in and around one of these bases. Much of it, in fact, does not revolve around the monsters, but around the personal dynamic between two men: Clent, the commander of the base, and Penley, formerly one of his colleagues, and now surviving in the icy wastes outside. The human story is that of Clent gradually realising that he had dismissed Penley's expertise too readily, and admitting him back into the base. At the story's climax, it's Penley's expertise with the ioniser, rather than Clent's, that saves the day.

That, however, is a long way off when, early on, one of the Base's scientists discovers what seems to be the body of an armoured warrior entombed in the ice nearby. The body of the warrior is brought back and slowly defrosted. By now, the Doctor and his companions have arrived, and the Doctor argues that the warrior cannot be human, since it has electronic components embedded in its head. It soon becomes clear that this creature is one of a Martian race known as the Ice Warriors, that there are more of them buried deeper in the ice, and that they also have a spaceship in the glacier which they want to reactivate.

It has to be said that a great deal of the appeal of *The Ice Warriors* lies in an extremely effective production. The creatures themselves have costumes crafted out of fibreglass so that they do indeed appear impregnable. The fibreglass is sculpted and ridged, however, to suggest a creature like a crocodile, suggesting without saying directly that these creatures are reptilian in origin. This hint is picked up by those playing the parts of the Ice Warriors, particularly Bernard Bresslaw (of *Carry On* movie fame) as their leader Varga. He adopts a sibilant, hissing delivery that both evokes a snake's hissing and suggests that the Ice Warriors are uncomfortable in Earth's atmosphere.

The script and the performances also combine to give the Ice Warriors a strongly martial culture. Varga and his band have the camaraderie of soldiers who have served together for many years. They fight for each other, and are visibly affected when one of them dies. The whole enterprise of trying to rescue their ship is a collective one. But they are also willing to put other creatures at risk to achieve their ends, and it's in order to safeguard the humans at the base that the Doctor ends up opposing them. The ways in which they evoke snakes also evoke that creature's mythical deceptiveness, though not as strongly as in the stories featuring the Mara (Chapter 31).

Their eventual defeat only arrives when their plan to free their spacecraft threatens the whole of the base and therefore the land it's holding back the ice from. Creatures of ice end up being defeated by heat, with the base's ioniser, now in Penley's hands, being used against them.

The Seeds of Death is a more conventional alien invasion story, and though the Ice Warriors are as visually impressive as before, it's not nearly as memorable. It's set in a near-future where space travel has been rendered obsolete by a system called T-Mat, which provides instant matter transmission across the Earth or between the Earth and the Moon. An Ice Warrior invasion fleet is poised to strike at the Earth, and before they do so they capture the T-Mat system and use it to distribute spores which will spread across Earth removing the oxygen from the atmosphere. The Doctor and his companions are required to recover the lost art of space travel in order to reach the stricken T-Mat stations and turn back the Ice Warriors.

In terms of the mythos of the Ice Warriors, *The Seeds of Death* does introduce one complication to the picture already shown. In addition to the warriors themselves, who appear much as in their debut, we're also introduced to another grouping within the species, the Ice Lords. These seem to be an officer caste, lacking the weapons or the great height of the warriors, and commanding them in battle. This distinction, between the officers and the ranks, is one replicated in *Warriors of the Deep* (Chapter 21), where the Silurians are seen in command of their 'brother' Sea Devils.

The Curse of Peladon marks one of the most interesting uses of monsters in the series' history. It occurs mid-way through the Jon Pertwee era, when the Doctor is making his first halting steps in using the TARDIS despite the Time Lords' blocks on his knowledge of its function. He and his companion, Jo, arrive on the dark and windswept planet of Peladon, where the king is overseeing a difficult political debate, essentially one of change versus stasis. Should Peladon, which is depicted as being a relatively primitive, almost feudal, society join the larger group of the Galactic Federation? Given that the story was broadcast around the time of the UK's admission to the

European Economic Community (as it then was), there's an obvious political subtext here. As the Doctor arrives, a number of aliens have gathered to try to influence Peladon's decision. Among them are several Ice Warriors. When a series of 'accidents' occur, causing suspicious deaths, the Doctor's first suspicions fall on the Ice Warriors. But they turn out to be innocent, and indeed to be loyal supporters of the Doctor's actions. The real villains are forces of conservatism within the Peladon court who wish to block accession to the Federation at any cost. In this story, the Ice Warriors' culture of military values is seen from another side. Their loyalty and ferocity, as well as their skill at fighting, become formidable assets when used in a good cause.

If *The Curse of Peladon* was a rare occasion when Doctor Who played its monsters against type, *The Monster of Peladon* reverts to type. Again, it's set on Peladon, some decades after the earlier story, and again there's a political problem that can be easily read as a parable of contemporary events. The premise is that Peladon is a source of the valuable mineral trisilicate, but that tunnelling under the royal palace has been disrupted because of visions of the semi-mythical royal beast Aggedor. Trisilicate is a vital ingredient in supplies for a war the Federation is currently waging against Galaxy Five. So the miners are refusing to work, an obvious parallel of the industrial unrest in the UK mining industry around the same time. Again, there's a Federation delegation on the planet, including an Ice Warrior named Azaxyr. Though his purpose appears to be to aid the Federation, Azaxyr's real role is as a supporter of Galaxy Five. Along with a human collaborator, Eckersley, he is conspiring to disrupt the flow of trisilicate.

Azaxyr is the first Ice Warrior in the series to indulge in what might be seen as treachery. It's a portrayal that goes very much against the way the creatures have been depicted up to this point. And although *The Monster of Peladon* is not a popular story, certainly it's over-long and drably directed, Azaxyr is one of the more interesting features in it. Above all, his presence indicates that the Ice Warriors are creatures who can choose how they act. If they can choose to be benevolent and honourable, as in *The Curse of Peladon*, they can also

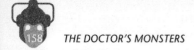

choose to be deceptive, as here. These four stories take the Ice Warriors progressively away from what made them most distinctive in the first place, such as the reptilian overtones of Bresslaw's performance. In the process, though, they make the creatures more human, more nuanced and less monstrous. Of all the monsters discussed in this book, they are the ones I'd find most fascinating to see more of.

THE 'MARTIANS' (1970)

I t's one of the odder paradoxes of the Jon Pertwee era that, although the Doctor's attachment to UNIT is supposed to be about him helping to prevent alien invasion, relatively few of the UNIT stories are actually about that. In Pertwee's first season, only the first story (*Spearhead from Space*, see Chapter 1) is clearly about that. The other three stories describe the Doctor's encounter with the Silurians (Chapter 11), the Primords (Chapter 4) and the strange Martians encountered in *The Ambassadors of Death*, none of them really constituting a conventional invasion.

The Ambassadors of Death has as its premise an idea that Doctor Who toyed with a couple of times over the years, a British-based space programme. However implausible this might be, for the most part it's rendered here with gritty realism. Onscreen, the story is credited as being written by David Whitaker, the series' very first script editor. However, as with so many of the stories discussed in this volume, it results from something of a behind-the-scenes production crisis. Whitaker's scripts were originally intended to be used during the reign of Pertwee's predecessor, Patrick Troughton. The final version was extensively rewritten, particularly by

Malcolm Hulke. They certainly have the distinctive moral complexity that Hulke's work often embodied.

As the story starts, a recovery mission is in progress to detect what has happened to Mars Probe Seven, which landed on the red planet some months ago. The probe was detected flying back to Earth, but provided no radio communication or other response to suggest that its astronauts were still alive. The recovery mission docks with the original probe, but as the connecting airlocks are opened there is a piercing sound, heard not just by the onboard astronauts but on Earth as well. The Doctor, watching a television broadcast of the rescue, is not merely disturbed by the sound but seems to recognise it. He and his companion, Liz, set off for the centre coordinating the space flight. Once there, they discover that the rescue capsule has also become incommunicado, and a further rescue is plotted. They also undertake, with the Brigadier, a triangulation of the signal that so disturbed them earlier. It seems to be 'centred', it's not clear how, on an abandoned warehouse near to Mission Control.

Once the Brigadier reaches the warehouse, the story takes the first of its several strange tonal shifts. We've been shown a group of men in a back room at the warehouse, who seem to be responsible for the signal rather than an extraterrestrial source. The Brigadier and his soldiers are fired on by these men, in a full-blown action sequence that sits very oddly with the sorts of cosmic horrors invoked at the start of the story. Some of the men are captured and marched off for interrogation, but enough of them remain alive to set off a self-destruct mechanism in their equipment.

But the end of the first episode returns to the disquieting idea that began it: silence. Repeated radio signals to the Mars capsules meet with no reply, nor can the astronauts be seen. The recovery capsule does, though, begin to make for Earth. It touches down in the south of England, and staff from the control centre go to try to recover the astronauts. But the capsule cannot be opened, and so it is instead transported on the back of a lorry to the space centre. Before it can get there, though, the lorry is ambushed by troops, seemingly part of the same force who were in the warehouse. By the time the capsule has been lost and recovered, the three astronauts inside are gone.

We see the astronauts first at the base of General Carrington, the man behind the attack at the warehouse and the hijacking of the convoy. They are still in their spacesuits, lying supine in a sealed chamber, having received massive doses of radiation on their journey back to Earth. Back at the space centre, Carrington is introduced to the Doctor as part of the establishment, the head of 'the newly-formed space security department'. He is also a former astronaut, having travelled on one of the Mars missions before this. He explains to the Doctor some of the thinking behind what has gone on. He believes that the most recent Mars mission encountered a new kind of radiation which could be 'self-sustaining'. If it was allowed to spread unchecked, it could spread across Earth like a plague.

So the story is not about the Martians so much as the effect the Martians have on the humans around them. The Martians are, in fact, a huge absence in the story, experienced almost always by report, most obviously Carrington's report of his traumatic encounter with them. This encounter, not seen onscreen, is the incident that precipitates the whole story. Carrington's xenophobia becomes a pathology which, due to his power and influence, shapes everything else. Despite that, though, we're made to see his side of things. Thanks to John Abinieri's performance as Carrington, we're made to see the horror that could result from an encounter with something that alien.

Moreover, the story recapitulates that horror in the visions of the space suited aliens that are, perhaps, its most enduring image. Because of their utter blankness, they represent just what Carrington feared most: the unknown, the other. This is a model of thinking that can be applied to many other groups. In a different context, Carrington's fear of the other might express itself as racism. Hence, for instance, Carrington's fear that the astronauts' presence could result in some kind of contamination of Earth, much as racist arguments claim that the presence of foreign cultures will contaminate the purity of the status quo.

The difference required by a science fiction setting for this story is that the Martians must remain, in the end, ineradicably different. Whatever else the story leads to, it's not a permanent rapprochement between humans and Martians. (It's worth noting, also, that these Martians seem to be unrelated to the Ice Warriors, who also come from the red planet.) For a story that is a biting critique of unthinking prejudice against the other, many of its most characteristic moments come from that fear. The space suited aliens, advancing with the sun behind them, bringing death to whoever gets in their way is one of the series' most memorable images. Even if the aliens have been coerced into acting as they do, they do unarguably kill people. So it could be said that *The Ambassadors of Death* is a story that has its cake and eats it, that exploits and critiques fear of the other.

The subject of contacts with creatures that are perceived as the other is a huge topic in both science fiction (see, for instance, MacLeod, 2005) and in anthropology (see, for instance, Bhabha, 1994), and a subject I can only touch on here. The central point I'd make, though, is that these encounters are often best understood as reflecting back on the people who are our viewpoint. In the case of *The Ambassadors of Death*, General Carrington is obviously an extreme case, but not an isolated one. The aliens are variously quarantined, feared and misunderstood by other humans. Although it doesn't show the process, the story makes it clear that reaching any proper understanding between the humans and the Martians will be a protracted and difficult process. This may be partly why the question of what happens next in this relationship was never addressed in the series; fear is very easy to make storyable, slow detente less so. As much as anything, *The Ambassadors of Death* is a story about how it might be possible to get past fear, and why it might be worthwhile.

THE TOCLAFANE (2007)

In many of the previous chapters, I've made the argument that some monsters are presented as having chosen their monstrosity or, at the very least, able to choose not to be monsters. This is emphatically not the case with the Toclafane, whose nature is one of the cruellest pieces of script-structuring in the series' history.

The set up for the creation of the Toclafane is the episode *Utopia* (2007), in which the Doctor finds himself at the very end of the universe's history, on one of the last planets surviving as all the stars go out. This planet is inhabited by a last colony of humans, whose base also contains a vast rocket ship which, they hope, will take them to a fabled place called Utopia. The Doctor arrives and swiftly meets with their resident scientist, Professor Yana. Over the course of the episode, he and Yana fix the rocket, but his presence also awakes in Yana memories of a past life, as the Master. The climax of the episode, as the rocket takes off for Utopia, also sees Yana opening the fob watch that contains his identity as the Master. Although he is shot by his assistant, the Master makes it into the Doctor's TARDIS, in which he regenerates, and which he then steals, leaving the

Doctor and his companions seemingly stranded at the end of the universe.

The start of the next episode, *The Sound of Drums*, fixes the immediate problem, the Doctor and his companions, Martha and Captain Jack, get back to contemporary Earth via the use of a time transportation bracelet owned by Jack. But, once there, they find that the Master has installed himself as the UK's Prime Minister, and has announced the impending arrival of a new alien species. These are the Toclafane, whom we are shown attacking a journalist who gets too close to discovering the Master's real plan. Each Toclafane is a floating metal sphere, about 18 inches in diameter, with weapons (guns and blades of various kinds) concealed in its body. They seem friendly with, and subservient to, the Master, and chatter to each other in childlike voices. They are also eager to murder on his behalf. At the climax of the episode, the Master welcomes the full contingent of six billion Toclafane down onto Earth, where at his command they commence killing a tenth of the population. The Master also captures and incapacitates the Doctor and Jack, leaving only Martha on Earth to observe the devastation and try to fight back.

The following episode, *The Last of the Time Lords*, picks up a year after this apocalypse. The Doctor and Jack are still held by the Master, who has been building a fleet of starships to create and perpetuate a new Time Lord empire. Humanity clearly lives in a state of terror under the Master and the Toclafane, but up until this point Martha has not been captured. Talking with the Master, the Doctor asks what the Toclafane are: It seems that stories of them were a little like stories of the bogeyman when they were children on Gallifrey. The Master clearly knows but isn't saying, 'If I told you, Doctor, your hearts would break.'

Meanwhile, Martha is on the point of discovering the answer to this very question. A scientist has captured a 'comatose' Toclafane, having observed that they can be neutralised by certain conditions similar to lightning. Inside is a mummified, shrivelled human head, kept alive by life support systems within the sphere. These, it's clear, are the remains of the humans seen in *Utopia*. The Master used the Doctor's

TARDIS to return to the far future, and created the Toclafane. The rift seen at the end of *The Sound of Drums* was, in a sense, bringing the Toclafane back home.

Throughout these two episodes, the Doctor's TARDIS has been serving the Master as a 'Paradox Machine', cannibalised to hold in place the elaborate temporal engineering needed to enable all this. When, at the end of the episode, the Master is defeated and the Paradox Machine destroyed, the events of the last year are rolled back as if they never happened. The tenth of the world's population killed by the Master are returned to life, his other crimes against the Earth's population are unmade and the Toclafane are returned to the end of the universe, presumably to remain there permanently.

When I said earlier that the script-structuring that created the Toclafane was cruel, I meant it in two senses. The first was that, unlike so many of the monsters I've discussed earlier, their transformation into a monstrous form was not their fault. The humans seen in *Utopia* are very deliberately positioned as hopeful, enterprising, energetic. One would be glad to see them surviving at the end of the universe, and their final flight to Utopia is filled with optimism. Instead, Utopia is a false dream, a confection of the Master's, where they are made into the Toclafane. The irony entailed in the name 'Utopia' is heavy enough as it is. The second sense is that, in the Toclafane, the Master has finally created what he had been seeking in many previous adventures, a human race subject to his will. They are his servants, nothing more, and the story seems to be saying that they have no more free will than he wants them to have. When the Master is defeated and the vast reset button of the Paradox machine is activated, they are swept out of sight and out of mind. For a series that, in so many of its stories, rewards human persistence and ingenuity, it's a savage way to treat the Doctor's favourite species. The Toclafane have no future, no choice and no hope.

THE CHEETAH-PEOPLE (1989)

Survival (1989) was the last story of Doctor Who's original run, and one of the most complex and interesting stories it ever presented. It begins with the Doctor and his companion, Ace, returning to Ace's home in Perivale, a dull suburb of London. The place seems mysteriously deserted, with many of Ace's friends having vanished. But a weird suburban apathy pervades the place, and no one seems to care about these missing people. (As one of Ace's friends explains to her, 'That's what they said. Either you were dead or gone to Birmingham.')

What's really going on is a series of abductions of locals by cat-like humanoids. They take the humans to their own, unnamed planet, a barren desert world. There, the cat-creatures, the Cheetah-people, engage in the pleasures of the hunt, killing those humans they catch and so brutally enacting the idea of survival of the fittest. Much about the Cheetah-people is mysterious such as how they achieve the abductions (visually, they just happen in a flash of light), the nature of their civilisation and their symbiosis with their planet. It's clear, though, that being on their world affects people in more than psychological ways.

Before the story reaches the Cheetah-people's planet, a series of arguments have been presented about the usefulness of seeing the world solely in terms of survival of the fittest. Ace's old youth club has been taken over by a martial arts trainer called Paterson, who preaches the virtues of self-defence as the only way to survive in the world, 'I reckon the only thing you can do is teach [young people] to fight. That way, they'll fight or go under. Half of them go under anyway round here. Can't save 'em. Wasters.'

It's worth remembering that, when this story was made and broadcast, Margaret Thatcher was still British Prime Minister. *Survival* can be seen as one of the most direct assaults *Doctor Who* ever made on a political belief system, in this case, the creed of self-reliance unmediated by other kinds of support from society.

Earlier on in the story, the Doctor finds himself in an ordinary shop, where he overhears an old joke: 'There are these two blokes, right? In a tent, in the jungle. It's really dark, and they hear this terrible noise outside the tent. This terrible roaring noise. And one bloke turns to the other bloke and says 'Did you hear that? That was a lion.' And the other bloke, he doesn't say anything. He just starts putting on his running shoes. The first bloke turns to him and says, 'What are you doing? You can't outrun a lion.' The bloke turns to him and says, 'I don't have to outrun the lion...'' The Doctor thinks the joke is 'very clever... if you don't mind losing your friend. But what happens when the next lion turns up?'

The point, of course, is that pursuing narrow self-interest only gets you so far and that it might even be a dead-end. All of these abstract arguments become literal when the story moves to the planet of the Cheetah-people. Ace, waiting idly in a playground, turns to see a shocking figure behind her, a cat-creature rearing up on horseback. She retreats from it, evidently terrified, but is too slow and is taken away in a flash to the alien world. By this time in the series' history, video technology had finally advanced enough to be able to create environments that seemed truly alien. Although the Cheetah-people's planet is that old standby, a sandpit in the Home Counties, the picture is altered enough to suggest an alien tint to the skies and the rumbling of distant volcanoes. The rider pursues Ace through this landscape until she encounters another human, evidently one taken from Earth some time before. The rider captures the other man and leaves Ace, who then meets Shreela, one of her friends missing on Earth.

Meanwhile, back on Earth, the Doctor makes a wrong move while trying to work out whether domestic cats have any link to the Cheetah-people. He is transported to the alien world along with Paterson, who has been following him as a potential 'nuisance'. They find themselves in a kind of Cheetah-people encampment. But in the grandest of the tents is a familiar face: the Master. He has been here for some while and is in the process of losing his nature to the planet. His eyes are becoming cat-like, and he seems to be developing a telepathic link with the Cheetah-people, whether on this world or Earth.

The choice of the Master to feature in this of all stories is a very interesting one. He is, after all, generally depicted in *Doctor Who* as a ruthless killer, perhaps warped by his obsession with the Doctor, but scarcely someone with scruples. Yet *Survival* shows him confronting the idea of having much of his nature stripped away to leave something far more primitive. It's undoubtedly Anthony Ainley's finest performance in the role, not least because it's the one in which his Master seems most likely to lose control of himself.

Throughout the course of the story's second episode, something similar is happening to Ace. She finds that she is skilled at surviving on this world, and perhaps even enjoys the hunt. The story doesn't flinch from depicting what this might mean; there are plenty of shots, for instance, of the Cheetah-people gnawing at chunks of red meat. Yet it also conveys, for want of a better word, the glamour of the Cheetah-people's life. Ace says at one point that she feels she could 'run forever' with them; separately, the Master says that 'this place bewitches you'. Ace also encounters, for the first time, a member of the Cheetah-people race who can speak. Up until this point, their capacity for the achievements of 'civilisation' hasn't been clear. They can ride horses and manipulate tools, and some of them wear necklaces or other adornments suggesting a sense of aesthetic beauty. But language, and the capacity it implies for empathy, is something new in the story. Before this question can be explored further, though, the Doctor arrives and warns Ace away from talking to the creature. He says, quite rightly, that the Cheetah-people are extremely dangerous. But there's an ambivalence, and therefore a complexity, to the way they're depicted. Both the Doctor and the Master say at various points that they're a 'fun-loving' species, and at one point a group of them toy with Paterson without killing him, despite clearly having the opportunity to do so.

The story starts introducing a certain amount of plottiness at this point. The Master tells the Doctor that the planet's volcanic convulsions aren't just routine, they're a signal of the planet's imminent disintegration. Perhaps predictably, Paterson's vaunted survival skills, he once went on an SAS survival course and was the only one to eat the worm stew, aren't so impressive when confronted with real threats. He finds himself leading a small group of humans on the alien world, but they soon turn against each other, each, as it were, putting on his or her running shoes. And a mechanism of escape from the planet is introduced: a creature that has spent enough time on the planet begins to take on the Cheetah-people's nature. It can then 'go home', and if its home was originally the Earth, that's where it will end up. Moreover, any creature touching it will also end up transported there. So, for the Doctor, the alarming prospect is that he will have to wait for one of the humans he knows to begin to become one of the Cheetah-people, and then use that person to escape. The cliffhanger to the second episode is that the likeliest candidate for this, her eyes already turning green and cat-like, is Ace.

The story's third and final episode mostly takes place on Earth, with the survivors of the Cheetah-people's planet bringing their newly-changed natures to this quiet setting. It is a less subtle and nuanced part of the story than the earlier episodes. That's especially true when the Doctor and a human controlled by the Master race towards each other on motorbikes in a kind of test-to-destruction of their survival instincts. The most interesting strand of the story is Ace's, as she continues to explore her cat-like nature on the alien world. The seductive nature of the Cheetah-people's life is superbly evoked. *Survival* is one of the best-directed stories the series ever had. We're repeatedly shown, rather than told, what's most important to them: their horses kicking up dust in the sunlight, the kinetic thrill of the chase, the sight of a lone figure in an otherwise desolate landscape. But at the same time, Ace rebels against the idea of eating and killing people, because the next person to be killed might be her.

The story's climax occurs with the Master and the Doctor returned to the Cheetah-people's planet, its disintegration accelerating. The Master's descent into his animal nature has gone even further, and he is consumed by nothing but his desire to kill the Doctor. As the planet rips itself apart around them, the Doctor gains the advantage, and has the chance to kill his old adversary. He too, like Ace before him, has acquired the Cheetah-people's cat-like eyes. But instead he gives up the advantage and the Master gains the upper hand. The Doctor shouts, 'If we fight like animals, we die like animals!', and finds himself back in Perivale. Meanwhile, Ace sees a lone rider ahead of her, a last reminder of the Cheetah-people, and then they return to the TARDIS, their adventures over for the moment.

This ending gains additional force from *Survival*'s place as the last *Doctor Who* story for many years. That the Doctor is returned to Earth suggests that this is, after all his years of wandering, something like his home. He too, like Ace, has clearly been tempted by the simplicities of life on the alien world. But his rejection of the chance to kill the Master is a reiteration of a moral principle seen throughout the series (most famously, perhaps, in *Genesis of the Daleks*). The idea of killing, and especially killing as an act of vengeance, is entirely alien to him.

So the question of what the Cheetah-people represent, what fragment of human nature they encapsulate, is a fairly simple one. What's more interesting, as I've tried to argue above, is the complexity with which this is conveyed. They are not unthinking animals, and not without a sense of beauty.

These ideas are given a final twist in the last episode. In a duel in Perivale, the Master stabs Kara, the one member of the Cheetah-people who had befriended Ace and spoken to her. As she falls down dying, Kara reverts to human form. The suggestion, though not made explicitly, is that many (and perhaps all) of the Cheetah-people on the alien world were originally human, that they were transformed into something more savage *by their environment*. This would explain the extent to which they retain their humanity, and their seeming affinity for Earth above all places.

As is often the case with monsters, the Cheetah-people's nature is underlined by the presence of at least one character who aspires to be like them. Initially, it looks like Paterson fulfils this role, with his simplistic view of survival. But sooner or later everyone transported to the alien planet, including the Doctor and the Master, fall into this category. *Survival* is very clear that what they need to do is resist this urge. As with the planet itself, the pure urge to survive leads only to self-destruction.

THE FENDAHL (1977)

In earlier chapters, on the Dæmons, the Sycorax and the Haemovores, I've suggested that *Doctor Who* has an ambivalent attitude about myths. On the one hand, it recognises that they provide good material for stories. On the other, however, the programme has a problem with fitting the essentially magic-based worldview of myth into its rational picture. The solution, as described in those earlier chapters, is to provide rational explanations for the seemingly magical. A similar approach is used in a couple of stories that rewrite classical myth as far-future science fiction, *Underworld* (1978) and *The Horns of Nimon* (1979–80). *Image of the Fendahl* (1977) fits into the same category, but with an unusual twist: some of the myths it draws on were already present in the culture, but some are new to the story.

Conventional wisdom has it that *Doctor Who*'s 'gothic' period covers its 12th to 14th seasons, broadcast from 1974 to 1977 and produced by Philip Hinchcliffe. After that, it's said, the emphasis on horror was reined back under the new producer, Graham Williams, and was replaced by increasingly broad humour. Yet *Image of the Fendahl*, the third story of the 15th season, is as disturbing as anything broadcast under

Hinchcliffe. Partly this is because Hinchcliffe's script editor, Robert Holmes, stayed on for the early part of Williams' tenure, including this story. It was Holmes who had provided many of the Hinchcliffe era's most graphic stories, such as *The Ark in Space* (see Chapter 17), *The Deadly Assassin* and *The Talons of Weng-Chiang*. It arguably makes far more sense to consider eras of *Doctor Who* not in terms of who was producing the series, but who was the dominant presence as script editor or writer.

The bulk of the story takes place at one of the series' favourite settings, the isolated scientific research establishment. In this case, it's a small lab in an ancient British house known as Fetch Priory. The team there is investigating a human skull discovered in Kenya which is, seemingly, 12 million years old – that is, 8 million years older than the known start of human life on Earth. There are four people working on the project: Dr Fendleman, who is funding the research from a private fortune, his assistant Max Stael, and two younger scientists who appear to be a couple, Thea Ransome and Adam Colby. Having dated the skull's age, their investigations involve some kind of scanning of the skull, the exact nature of the scans isn't explained, which causes it to glow and exercise a hypnotic effect, particularly on Thea.

At the same time as one of these experiments, we're shown a hiker walking alone at night through woods near the priory. He seems to be pursued by something unseen, and runs in increasing terror from it. Eventually, he stops, screams in terror, and falls to the ground. The next morning, Colby finds the corpse. There is no obvious cause of death, and despite the time of death being relatively recent, it soon begins to decompose. Fendleman resists telling the police about the death because of his fear that it will delay the research.

The Doctor and his companion, Leela, land in the TARDIS near to the priory. Though they are separated in the woods outside, the Doctor soon finds his way to the priory. There, he speaks with Adam about Thea, who has passed out on the floor after tampering with Fendleman's equipment. A glow suffuses her body, which also seems to be covered with creeping worm-like creatures. The Doctor remarks that these 'look like embryo Fendahleen to me'. This is a crucial moment in the story. Although the Doctor goes on to say that they are 'creatures from my own mythology', that is, he's not met them before, the point is that he recognises them. We sense that the diverse events that have happened so far, such as the glowing skull, the hiker's death and now Thea's transformation, will be subsumed under one explanation which the Doctor alone can provide.

The Doctor's subsequent conversation with Colby goes some way to providing this explanation. The Fendahleen perished when the 'fifth planet broke up' 12 million years ago. The remains of this planet are now the asteroid belt between Mars and Jupiter. Colby immediately seizes on this timing because it accords with the age of the skull. 'There are four thousand million people here on your planet, and if I'm right within a year there'll be just one left alive. Just one.' Before he can go further, though, Fendleman arrives with guards and sends the Doctor away to be locked up.

Meanwhile, Leela has found her way to a cottage in the woods where she meets a man named Jack Tyler. He drops dark hints about 'the old religion' practised around here, which his grandmother Martha is supposed to know about. These hints seem to point towards ideas of witchcraft, ideas reinforced by visuals of Tarot cards being turned over earlier in the same episode. We begin to suspect that this too may be part of the pattern that the Doctor hinted at earlier.

In an argument between Colby and Fendleman, we're given more ideas about the root cause of what's happening. Fendleman advances the suggestion that humanity did not originally evolve on Earth, that its origins stem from the alien traveller represented by the skull. He and Stael have also been X-raying the skull in secret, and have discovered a pentagram that seems to be 'part of the bone structure itself'. Fendleman believes it to be a kind of 'neural relay', and that this somehow has caused the human idea that the pentagram is a 'symbol for mystical energy and power' throughout history. Fendleman, like Thea, seems to be acting under the influence of a power not yet wholly on-stage. The Doctor explains a little more about the Fendahl: it survives and nourishes itself on the life force of anything it encounters. As he says later, in what may be the central line of the story, 'How do you kill death itself?'

At this point, about halfway through the story, it almost seems like *Image of the Fendahl* might be a kind of grand unified theory of human superstition. It might draw into its ambit, provide explanations for, almost any superstition it chose to, rationalising them as somehow descended from the Fendahleen incursion into prehistoric Earth. Inevitably, its realisation in the last episode or two is something of a letdown. Because television, like film, only steps away from being a naturalistic medium with great effort and cost, the Fendahl have to be somehow represented in the flesh, as it were. In this case, they're represented as giant green worms shuffling along the corridors of Fetch Priory. As the story's visual effects designer Colin Mapson notes in the DVD documentary 'After Image', the worms look so obviously phallic that he was worried they might not be suitable to broadcast. Even the addition of cobra-like flaps either side of the worm's head does not remove the problem, and Louise Jameson (Leela) says that the first time she saw one, she was unable to stop laughing for 15 minutes.

More back story about the Fendahl follows. The Fendahl did indeed inhabit the now-lost fifth planet of our solar system, but they were placed in a 'time loop' by the intervention of the Time Lords. This makes sense of the Doctor's reference to the Fendahl as part of the mythology when he was growing up on Gallifrey.

But there are still many intriguing turns to be unpicked in the story. Stael reveals himself as the true power among the team of scientists. He has constructed in the priory a room with a pentagram inscribed in the floor which he intends to use to allow the rebirth of the Fendahleen. He has also been nurturing a group of local cultists to assist in the rebirth. As the Doctor remarks, the name of Fetch Priory is not an accident, since 'Fetch' means an apparition, perhaps a common site around a fissure in time and space such as the Priory sits on. By the same token, Fendleman, now captured by Stael in the pentagram chamber, reveals his own self-knowledge:

that his name, 'man of the Fendahl', denotes the idea that he and his ancestors have been acting under the influence of the Fendahl for many years, culminating in this moment. It's interesting, in retrospect, to watch the human characters' actions in the story. Even when seemingly innocent, such as the early investigations of the skull, the scientists could have been acting under the influence of the Fendahl. Not least of the story's disturbing ideas is that even 'normal-seeming' people could not be exercising as much free will as they think.

In any case, the ritual to bring the Fendahl back now commences. Stael kills Fendleman, seemingly on a whim and, with Thea lying at the centre of the pentagram, begins the kind of incantation familiar from the 'black magic' works of Denis Wheatley. Thea is transformed into a golden-haired and golden-skinned being. This, the Doctor later explains, is the Fendahl 'Core'. The Fendahl is a gestalt organism comprising a core and 12 Fendahleen worms: the skull from which this all began was presumably also once part of a Fendahl core. Accordingly, the core kills Stael's cultists and begins transforming them into the full Fendahl organism. By now Stael realises the ritual has gone disastrously wrong. He asks the doctor to bring him a gun and kills himself, evidently deciding that self-inflicted death is better than death at the hands of the creature he has helped bring into being.

Another superstition now comes into play, the idea that apparitions of this kind are vulnerable to salt. Again, this turns out to have a basis in real life, and the Doctor and Leela are able to exploit the weakness to get past the Fendahl worms, reach the pentagram room and remove the skull. The Doctor has set the lap equipment to cause a 'controlled implosion' that will destroy the Priory. After a nightmarish race through its collapsing halls, he, Leela and a few others manage to escape. The Priory is destroyed, and the Fendahl with it. As the story ends, the Doctor says he is taking the skull off in the TARDIS, where he will drop it into a supernova. The evil, it seems, has been contained and normality restored.

So *Image of the Fendahl* is in part a story of possession, of humans being transformed into something else, like *Survival*.

It's also about forbidden scientific knowledge, like *Inferno*. And, as the summary above sets out, it rationalises the myths it depicts, almost too much. But its atmosphere is most like the classic horror stories of, say, the turn of the twentieth century. In particular, it's strongly reminiscent of stories of generational haunting like Arthur Machen's 'The Great God Pan' or M R James's 'The Ash Tree'. By focussing so overwhelmingly on events in Fetch Priory, it also sits in the related tradition of haunted house stories such as Edgar Allan Poe's 'The Fall of the House of Usher'. Hence the cathartic event that seems to break the curse at the end of the story is the destruction of the house, as in Poe, with fire purging the evil, as in the James.

As I've already suggested, the most disturbing thing about the story is not the monsters themselves, but the effect that their presence, or their anticipated presence, has on the humans – specifically, the team of four scientists. An early cue to this is the reaction to the hiker's body being found in the woods. Fendleman's wish to avoid involving the police in the death, even though no possible suspicion can be attached to him, is an indication that he's prepared to put his work above everything. Like so many other monsters in the series, the effect of the Fendahl is to make humans monstrous. The lucky ones, like Stael, realise what they have done.

THE MANDRELS (1980)

om Baker's penultimate season as the Doctor, produced by Graham Williams and script-edited by Douglas Adams, is not very highly regarded. It does contain, in the Williams/Adams-scripted *City of Death*, one unarguable classic, a free-wheeling time travel story set, and partly shot, in Paris. But many of the other stories are slight, jokey and hampered by budget restrictions. The scheduled climax of the season, a six-episode story by Adams called *Shada*, was dogged by industrial action at the BBC, and ended up as the only *Doctor Who* story to have begun but not completed filming. There was also an increasing trend of Baker's persona as the Doctor becoming more important than the stories. His peculiar and undeniable charisma too often eclipsed the jeopardy that should have driven the stories.

All of these criticisms apply to the season's fourth story, *Nightmare of Eden* (1979). And yet there are some ideas in the story that, despite the limitations of the production, are far more complex than usual for the series. The story begins in a human-dominated future, above the planet Azure. Two spaceships have a strange collision as a result of hyperspace travel: each partially melds with the other. One ship is a tourist liner, the Empress, and the other is a trade ship, the Hecate. The Doctor and Romana materialise shortly after the collision, and the Doctor, posing as a loss adjuster for the Empress's insurers, thinks that the initial problem is simply to separate the two. But he and Romana rapidly become interested in the work of one of the Empress's passengers, a zoologist named Tryst. He has the goal of cataloguing all life forms in the galaxy, and to this end has built a 'Continual Event Transmuter' machine. This CET machine stores and replays the life forms he has encountered, not merely in the sense of taking pictures of them, but actually recording and storing physical copies of them. It therefore leaves 'bald patches' on the planets Tryst has visited. As the Doctor says, it's just 'an electric zoo'. There's an obvious, though initially unstated, link with the discovery of the body of a crewmember who seems to have been mauled by some kind of animal.

A further plot thread concerns a drug called 'vraxoin' or 'zip', which seems to be widely used in this time and place. It is addictive and dangerous; the soporific state it induces frequently leads to death. It seems clear that one of the crewmembers is an addict, with potentially dangerous consequences for everyone else. The Doctor unambiguously condemns the drug: 'I've seen whole planets ravaged by it, while the merchants make fortunes'. The subject of drug addiction is only rarely broached in Doctor Who, and in no story is it as central as it is here.

The action of the story proper begins from the end of the first episode, when the Doctor opens a panel into one of the melded zones of the ships and a ferocious clawed creature reaches out to attack him. This is a Mandrel, and it's explained that they're among the creatures Tryst collected on his trip, in this case, to a planet called Eden. They were liberated from their home in the CET by the collision, and they progressively rampage through the ship. In a sense, the Mandrels aren't very different from Kroll: they don't speak or communicate at all, they seem nothing but hostile and deadly and they pop up in the story at any time the human characters need to be put in jeopardy.

But, also like Kroll, they have an origin story that's rather surprising. Towards the end of the story's third episode, one of the Mandrels is incinerated and reduced to a grey powder – raw Vraxoin. Tryst's cargo of Mandrels is, therefore, not just a set of animal specimens but, potentially, a huge store of a valuable drug. The last episode sees the Doctor arriving at the conclusion that Tryst is part of a Vraxoin-smuggling ring and trapping him and his collaborators.

So *Nightmare of Eden* is a story where the nonhuman monsters are deadly, but far from the most evil creatures. The Mandrels are, in a sense, too primitive to be evil. In rampaging round the ship and killing people they are merely following their nature, presumably shaped by the harsh environment of the jungle they come from. It's even possible to feel sorry for them, as it is for all zoo animals, trapped in a tiny patch of their native environment far away from home. This feeling is compounded by the way in which they're used by the humans. Tryst and his colleagues will end up burning all the Mandrels for their stored vraxoin.

As I said at the start, many of these ideas are obscured by the production. The spaceships look very dull and studio-bound, and the direction is extremely pedestrian. Some of the performances are weak too, Tryst in particular being played with a singularly unconvincing generic foreign accent. The Mandrels' costumes aren't terribly convincing either, being the kind of men-in-rubber-suits aliens where it's all too easy to see the seams.

But if there's one idea I'd latch onto about the story, it's the name of the Mandrels' home planet. 'Eden' has an obvious Biblical resonance, suggesting, as I argued above, that its inhabitants live in a state before good and evil. As in the story of Genesis, it's a human act that introduces those concepts to the world, in this case, Tryst's abduction of the Mandrels with drug profits in mind.

The science fiction critic John Clute has suggested, in another context, that 'Eden is always in the past tense' for us (Clute, 1995). That is, it's a state we may remember, or hear stories about, but can never return to. I want next to consider another story that presents an Eden disrupted by too much knowledge and too much thought.

THE MARA (1982, 1983)

For most of this book, the assumption has been that I am offering an interpretation of what a given monster represents. The story is one thing, and my interpretation is another, which may be more or less plausible given the evidence in the story. The two stories featuring the Mara, *Kinda* (1982) and *Snakedance* (1983) are rather different: it's very difficult to think of any other *Doctor Who* stories that are so overtly symbolic and freighted with *placed* meaning. The author of both of them, Christopher Bailey, has been explicit in interviews that this was his intent, though the author's intent is, of course, only one way to interpret a story. *Kinda* in particular is one of the most densely scripted stories the show ever broadcast. Discussion of it was central to one of the first serious academic studies of the series, Tulloch and Alvarado's *Doctor Who: The Unfolding Text* (1983).

Kinda takes place on the jungle world of Deva Loka. A human expedition has relatively recently arrived there and established a survival dome. The team are to assess the planet's suitability for human colonisation. But members of their group keep disappearing, and as they story starts only three of them are left: Todd, the science officer, and two security staff, the older Sanders and the younger Hindle. (In a wonderful coup of casting, Sanders is played by Richard Todd, probably most famous for his role in *The Dambusters*. Given that the part of Sanders amounts to a savage critique of the limitations of the military mind, Todd's commitment to the script is both eye-opening and admirable.)

The panic these incidents induce is at odds with what the planet seemed to promise, an Eden with a stable climate, perpetually fruiting trees and seemingly, no natural dangers. A native people, the Kinda, inhabit the jungle, but they are without speech and so assumed to be primitive. Todd, the only woman left among the dome crew, suspects they may be telepathic, but has not managed to establish communications with them.

Meanwhile, the TARDIS has landed in the jungle outside the dome. The Doctor and his companions, Tegan and Adric, find nearby an extraordinary artefact: a set of crystalline wind chimes hanging in the midst of the forest. Given that these chimes produce musical intervals that could not have happened by accident, the Doctor deduces that they must have been created by an intelligent species of some kind. Tegan falls asleep near to the Wind chimes while the Doctor and Adric explore further, and the story takes a turn into some very strange territory. We're shown what appears to be a dream sequence from Tegan's point of view. She finds herself in a black void, where she encounters ghostly figures who mock and cajole her. They doubt her existence and sanity, and one of them, Dukkha, seems to offer her a deal whereby she can return to the world. All she has to do is accept the transfer of a snake tattoo from Dukkha's arm to hers. Worn down eventually, she accepts, and wakes back on Deva Loka possessed by the Mara, an evil spirit.

Back at the dome, things have begun to fall apart. Sanders has left the dome in the 'Total Survival Suit' (TSS), a kind of one-person tank that's supposed to protect the user completely. In his absence, Hindle has taken command and moved further to the nervous breakdown that had already been likely. Meanwhile, it becomes apparent that the Kinda can indeed speak, but that speech is freighted with special significance for them. When one of the Kinda men, Aris, begins to talk, it's a mark of his possession by the Mara. Most of the information about the Mara is conveyed in a long scene between the Doctor and Panna, an old woman of the Kinda tribe, at the end of the third episode. In a truly visionary monologue, she depicts the wheel of civilisation, rising and falling, with the Mara at the root of the corruption that destroys societies, and glorying in the destruction. At the end of the speech (and the episode) she dies, leaving the Doctor with the problem of how to deal with the Mara. In a story so rich with symbolic meaning, it's no surprise that the answer to this question is a symbolic one. The Doctor reasons that the one thing evil cannot bear is the sight of itself. So he and the Kinda gather some huge mirrors from the dome and arrange them in a circle. They trick the possessed Aris into entering the circle and, once he has, close the circle so there's no way for him to escape. In this trap, the Mara has no option but to leave Aris. It manifests firstly in its natural form as a vast snake, and then vanishes, seemingly leaving the planet in peace. The humans in the dome have to rethink their ideas of Deva Loka as a primitive place they are entitled to take possession of, and the Doctor and his companions leave, though not without the sense that Tegan is permanently marked by her encounter with the Mara.

Throughout, this is a story that uses and pushes to the limit the kinds of video technology available in the early 1980s. So, for instance, Tegan's first encounter with the Mara is shown via a long zoom straight into her eye, which becomes the black void that the Mara inhabits. Despite being entirely shot in a studio, the jungle is mostly a convincing environment. The only weak point is the final appearance of the Mara as a giant snake that's rather too obviously a built prop rather than a living creature.

Snakedance is a more orthodox *Doctor Who* story both in its scripting and its presentation. It takes place on Manussa, the Mara's home planet. The planet is now largely occupied by humans, who tell themselves stories of the Mara's defeat many years ago. Indeed, the story of the Mara has now become ritualised and normalised: it's not exactly that the creature is a myth, but it's certainly not believed in as something that could return. The bulk of the story follows an attempt by the Mara to reconstitute itself through the ceremonial rituals marking its defeat. These rituals use tokens actually still charged with a great deal of power, notably a crystal which carries power to control human minds. This attempted return takes place partly through Tegan, who begins to fall under the creature's sway once again, and partly through Lon, an arrogant young aristocrat.

Far more than the first story, *Snakedance* is one in which the Doctor himself must go on a spiritual journey to understand and so defeat the Mara. This mostly happens through his discovery of, and subsequent conversations with Dojjen, a hermit with far more understanding than most of the Mara's nature. The lessons the Doctor must learn are very similar to those carried by Buddhism: a denial of the self and selfish needs, which, of course, are what the Mara represents. What *Snakedance* lacks is, I'd suggest, the simplicity of the images of *Kinda*. Here, for instance, there isn't anything as obviously evocative as the untouched jungle, the wheel of civilisation or the ring of mirrors. Manussa is a more 'civilised' place, and therefore not so easily rendered in terms of symbolism. What's constant across both stories is the sense that the Mara tempts and accentuates the characteristics of those already responsive to evil. Tegan, in the first story, takes a long time to be won over by the Mara, and the Kinda Aris is a far more natural home for the Mara's spirit. Similarly, in *Snakedance*, Lon is already filled with pride and hubris and sees the Mara's ascendancy as something that will also carry him to glory. As with the Fendahl, the Mara is defined as much as anything by what it does to others.

As I've said, there are so many layers of symbolism embodied in the Mara stories that it's almost impossible to pick one out. However, especially in the context of other stories I'd discuss in this book, I'd point especially to the way the creature uses language. Language is the means by which the Mara articulates what it wants, but it always speaks through others. When Aris is possessed by the Mara in *Kinda*, he achieves and uses the gift of speech, rather than telepathy as his fellow Kinda use. The use of language, especially in the context of Deva Loka's Eden, is a kind of Fall. In Snakedance, we're surrounded by characters who use language to *avoid* knowledge. The curator Ambril, or the showman in the market, talk about the Mara but fail to realise its true nature. The Doctor, following Dojjen, achieves the knowledge he needs by means of silence. This is a radical message in a series as filled with talk as *Doctor Who*. It perhaps also accounts for why these two stories are seen as atypical, 'adult', and perhaps too complex for the series. At the very least, they're one of *Doctor Who*'s most courageous attempts to push back against what a *Doctor Who* story is 'supposed' to be like.

THE DALEKS IV (2005–10)

O ne of the questions that has arisen with almost every
race of creatures discussed in this book is to what
extent its members are depicted as having free will
rather than being bound by their genetic, cultural and racial
backgrounds into set patterns of behaviour.

In my view, there is no more sophisticated, gripping or
thought-provoking treatment of this question in the series'
history than Robert Shearman's *Dalek* (2005). Sharing some
plot elements in common with Shearman's audio play *Jubilee*
(2003), it takes place a few years in the future in an underground compound in Utah in the USA. As the revived series'
first story depicting the Daleks, it was inevitably the subject
of high expectations, and it seems that Shearman and the
production team took it as an opportunity to reinvent the
Daleks from the ground up.

In the episodes of the 2005 series before *Dalek*, it had been
established that the Doctor's planet, Gallifrey, was destroyed
in something called the Time War, seemingly shortly before
the series began. *Dalek* fills in much of the rest of this background: the Time War was ultimately between the Time
Lords and the Daleks and was a final conflict with the whole

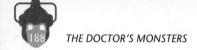

of creation at stake. The Doctor seems to have had some role in ending the war, and did so in a way that removed all trace of both the Time Lords and Daleks from creation.

Hence the Doctor's horror when he encounters, captured in the Utah compound, a Dalek. It was found by van Statten, the billionaire genius who owns the compound, after it fell to Earth screaming some years ago. Van Statten is a collector of what he thinks are alien artefacts, but it's clear that he's an undiscriminating collector; he wants to *own* rather than to understand. The Dalek is the jewel of his collection, but despite being attacked, in effect, tortured, by van Statten's operatives, it has revealed nothing of its secrets. It only properly comes to life when the Doctor is thrown into the cell where it is kept chained:

> DALEK: Keep back!
> THE DOCTOR: What for? What're you going to do to me? Because if you can't kill, then what are you good for...Dalek? What's the point of you? You're nothing! What are you doing here? What the hell are you here for?
> DALEK: I am waiting for orders.
> THE DOCTOR: What does that mean?
> DALEK: I am a solider, I was bred to receive orders.
> THE DOCTOR: Well, you're never going to get any. Not ever.
> DALEK: I DEMAND ORDERS!
> THE DOCTOR: Well they're never gonna +come+! Your race is dead! You all burned, all of you. Ten million ships on fire. The entire Dalek race, wiped out in one second.
> DALEK: You lie!
> THE DOCTOR: I watched it happen. I +made+ it happen!
> DALEK: You destroyed us?
> THE DOCTOR: I had no other choice.
> DALEK: And what of the Time Lords?
> THE DOCTOR: Dead. They burnt with you. The end of the last great Time War. Everyone lost.

This side of the Doctor, vengeful, furious, destructive, is one hardly ever seen in the series before. Christopher Eccleston's superb performance as the Doctor is never better here, and he goes on to tell the Dalek he'll give it what it truly deserves: 'Exterminate'. And he flicks the switch to electrocute the creature. Although he's soon captured, the implication is clear: In a moment like this, the Doctor is not so different from a Dalek himself.

While Van Statten is interrogating the Doctor, Rose visits the creature in its cell. The Dalek, using the kind of cunning seen in *The Power of the Daleks*, tricks her into touching its shell. Her DNA helps to regenerate the creature, and it begins to come to life again. Although she flees the cell, and soldiers attempt to hold off the Dalek, their attempts are futile. Most of the episode follows the Dalek's progress through the base, progressively killing the soldiers and working its way towards the surface. It's never been so clear how formidable a single Dalek is, partly also thanks to a redesign of the creatures that makes them look vastly more solid and impregnable. By the time the Dalek reaches the compound's top level, the Doctor has ransacked Van Statten's collection to find something that might serve as a weapon against it, not least since it has been holding Rose hostage. But when he encounters the creature, he finds that it seems to be changing. It has not killed Rose, despite opportunities to do so, and rather than advancing forward it opens its casing so that the mutant inside can experience the sunlight. Rose angrily stops the Doctor from shooting the creature and, as he realises where his actions have taken him, the following exchange takes place:

DALEK: Why do we survive?
THE DOCTOR: I don't know.
DALEK: I am the last of the Daleks.
THE DOCTOR: You're not even that. Rose did more than regenerate you. You've absorbed her DNA: You're mutating.
DALEK: Into what?
THE DOCTOR: Something new. I'm sorry.
ROSE: Isn't that better?
THE DOCTOR: Not for a Dalek.
DALEK: I can feel. So many ideas. So much darkness. Rose, give me orders. Order me to die.
ROSE: I can't do that.

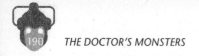

DALEK: This is not life. This is sickness. I shall not be like you. Order my destruction! Obey! +Obey+! O-BEY!
ROSE: Do it.
[*the Dalek self destructs*]

There's almost too much in this scene to comment on. The Dalek's experience of its body as 'sickness', for instance, mirrors what we might feel seeing the mutant, but there's also a sense of how painful this self-knowledge is. The scene has throughout it a tension between the Dalek's inherent nature (as created by its mutation and the machine it inhabits) and the new self it is evolving into. The final irony is that, as it progresses away from its Dalek nature, it still needs that nature: the final shouts of 'Obey!' are much more Dalek-like than its previous dialogue. At the same time, the Doctor is learning from what he sees. His rage at the Dalek when they first met is replaced by, if anything, a kind of fellow-feeling, a recognition of how much they share as survivors of the Time War.

The subsequent stories in the revived series using the Daleks were, it has to be said, far less interesting explorations of their mythos. The finale of the 2005 season, *Bad Wolf/The Parting of the Ways*, was unashamedly a spectacular. It featured a full-blown invasion of a far-future Earth by half a million Daleks. For the first time, the technology available to the programme allowed this to be shown on screen in something like its full scale. The finale did, however, add one new twist to the existing story of the Daleks. This race of Daleks had been created from human flash by the Emperor Dalek, who managed to escape the Time War.

The human-based Daleks we see now worship the Emperor as a kind of god, a role which the Emperor is only too happy to play. For the first and only time, the Dalek hierarchy is not a military one, but something like a theology. The Doctor is 'the heathen', the Daleks are the Emperor's 'angels' and so on. Russell T Davies, author of these episodes, is on record with his own atheist beliefs, but he clearly also has a kind of fascination with religion, as witness his ITV drama *The Second Coming*. In the context of the Daleks, religion becomes something fundamentalist and pathological, a toxic dogma.

The subsequent season finale, *Army of Ghosts/Doomsday*, was also written by Davies, and also featured the Daleks. In this case, though, four of them arrive on contemporary Earth and encounter an army of Cybermen. The immediate question the episode raises is the old playground debate: Who would win in a fight between Daleks and Cybermen? The answer, it quickly becomes apparent, is the Daleks would win easily. More interesting is the nature and status of these four Daleks. They have, uniquely among the species, individual names. The Doctor recognises them as part of 'the cult of Skaro', a secret group that was required to 'think the unthinkable' about the nature of the Daleks. This idea is not much explored in this story, but all four of these Daleks escape, and it's a concept left to be explored.

The Dalek story in the 2007 season, *Daleks in Manhattan/Evolution of the Daleks*, ought by rights to be one of the series' highlights. It marks a very deliberate return to the territory of *Evil of the Daleks*. After their defeat in *Doomsday*, the four Daleks of the Cult of Skaro initiated an 'Emergency Temporal Shift' and retreated to Depression-era New York. There, believing themselves to be the last Daleks in existence, they begin a programme of genetic experimentation. In the first instance, this is just to provide themselves with a compliant workforce. At the end of the first episode, though, their real plan is revealed: They have turned Dalek Sec into a 'human-Dalek hybrid', in order to see if they can survive outside their casings. However, the other three members of the Cult become increasingly concerned about this move, and the main plot of the second episode is taken up with their gradual turning against Dalek Sec, to the point where they ultimately execute him. At the same time, Dalek Sec, like his predecessors in *Evil of the Daleks*, has been discovering that human nature is very much at odds with what he has believed up to now as a Dalek. In a sense, this is the same debate as was conducted in Shearman's *Dalek*. However, this story lacks *Dalek*'s insight of the Doctor as a kind of mirror image of the Daleks. Instead, in a key scene in a New York theatre, David Tennant's Doctor is able to confront the surviving Daleks from a position of unquestioned moral authority. All the ambivalence of *Dalek* (or, indeed, *Evil of the Daleks*) is lost.

In addition, *Daleks in Manhattan* is another case of the series overreaching itself. Although some background plate shots were taken in New York, the body of the story was made on location in Wales. There are scarcely any New York street scenes, and a park in Wales doubles very unconvincingly for Central Park. Although the actors and other participants do their best, the Art Deco design is especially effective, it's a story that almost totally fails to convey the atmosphere of the place it's set in. It also relies, even more than most *Doctor Who* stories, on science that seems to be made up on the hoof. In this case, the climax of the story relies on the idea that, since the Doctor is clinging on to the tower of the Empire State Building when lightning strikes, his 'Time Lord DNA' gets transmitted into the Daleks' human-hybrid slaves. In general, in this phase of Doctor Who, 'DNA' fulfils the same properties of scientific entity that will do anything as did static electricity in the David Whitaker era.

The 2008 Dalek story, *The Stolen Earth/Journey's End*, continues the idea of genetic experimentation. In this case, the experiments stem from Davros, thought lost in the Time War but in fact rescued from that maelstrom by Dalek Caan, following his Emergency Temporal Shift at the end of *Evolution of the Daleks*. Davros has created a new race of Daleks from his own flesh, and created a space station enclave for them ('the Crucible') from which he intends to launch a universe-destroying 'reality bomb'. His defeat at the hands of the Doctor and his companions is predictable, but the story does introduce an interesting dynamic between him and the Daleks. He is relegated to a kind of laboratory/basement on the Crucible; as the Doctor says, he is their 'pet'. And, if nothing else, Julian Bleach's performance as Davros exceeds in intensity even Michael Wisher's as the original in *Genesis of the Daleks*.

The Daleks have a cameo, a telling one, in *The Waters of Mars*, David Tennant's penultimate story as the Doctor. That story revolves around the survival of the first human colonists on Mars, midway through the twenty-first century. Their leader, Captain Adelaide Brooke, was caught up as a girl in the Dalek invasion of Earth shown in *Journey's End*. Waiting at home for her father to return, she looked out of the window and saw a Dalek approaching. It looked in at her, through her, but, for no obvious reason, refrained from killing her. That encounter set her on the path that led to her commanding the Mars mission: The Dalek's otherworldly nature impelled her to go and discover more worlds beyond Earth. It's an encounter playing not on the Daleks as something terrible, but simply as something alien and iconic. The mere sight of them carries so much meaning that they need to say nothing to add to it. Their appearance in *The Waters of Mars* carries as much force as it does because of the unique place they occupy in our culture.

This is reinforced in their subsequent appearance, in *Victory of the Daleks* (2010). The premise is almost irresistible: Winston Churchill calls in the Doctor because he has had an offer of help from the Daleks for the fight against the Nazis in World War II. For the first half of the story, the Daleks are meek, helpful and subservient, offering cups of tea and blasting down German fighter planes on command. The story very deliberately harks back to the cunning that the creatures exhibited in *Power of the Daleks*. At the midpoint, though, the true shape of the story is revealed: The small contingent of Daleks helping Churchill are indeed playing for time. They have a spaceship near Earth, which contains a 'progenitor ark' of original Dalek genetic material. The Doctor's arrival and intervention in the story is proof to the progenitor ark that these Daleks, so much modified over the years, are indeed descendents of the original Kaled strain. With this 'testimony', it sets off the creation of a 'new Dalek paradigm', redesigned Daleks very much larger and more colourful than those in the 2005–8 era. They were very deliberately based on the more extravagant creatures first seen in the spin-off movie *Doctor Who and the Daleks* (1965).

On the face of it, then, this is a story that returns to the roots of the Dalek mythos: It deals with racial purity and the Daleks' horror at those who are unlike them. (The new paradigm Daleks' first act is to exterminate the older ones, even before they threaten the Doctor.) The new Daleks escape and are, it seems, set to become a persistent presence in the *Doctor Who* universe in the same way that they were before the Time War. But this is one of those occasions when thinking of *Doctor Who* just as a TV series is damagingly limiting. At the moment, for instance, *Doctor Who* is also a website, a series of books and DVDs, an exhibition at Kensington Olympia, a magazine, audio adventures and so on. It's also, of course, a series of toys modelled after characters and monsters such as the Daleks. The remaking of the Daleks in this story also enabled the remaking of those toys. Functionally, at least, the new Daleks sound almost exactly the same as the old ones, and every indication is that they will behave in the same way. But, like a logo, they are a symbol that can be revised but still mean the same. The Daleks now are not so much monsters as a brand.

THE SILENTS (2011)

When I began writing this book a few years ago, the quotation I chose at the start from Christopher Bidmead's *Logopolis* was something of a joke. I had half-seriously asserted on a couple of occasions that the Doctor was engaged in an endless quest against abstract nouns – against evil, say, or war or artificiality. Little did I guess that, as I was finishing the book, the Doctor would spend an entire season of adventures fighting an abstract noun.

The seeds for this were sown in the 2010 season of the programme, Matt Smith's first in the role. At the end of his first adventure, *The Eleventh Hour*, he was warned of two mysterious events in his future: 'The Pandorica will open. Silence will fall.' At various points during the season, for instance at the end of *The Vampires of Venice*, there were hints of what this Silence might be: a universe stripped of all life in which no voice might be heard. This threat seemed, at the end of the season, to be averted. A complex trap was laid for the Doctor in which he was placed within an inescapable prison, the Pandorica, while his TARDIS was mysteriously caused to explode. Inevitably, both of these were rectified in the season finale, but with a mystery remaining: that 'the Silence' appeared to be more than just an abstraction, and to have caused the destruction of the TARDIS.

In the opening story of the 2011 season, *The Impossible Astronaut/The Day of the Moon*, we find out at least part of the answer, thanks to some word play. In the USA of 1969, we're introduced to creatures called The Silents. So, perhaps, 'The Silence' was a kind of mishearing? They're tall, clad in dark business suits, but with elongated faces that resemble those of the extraterrestrials many UFO-spotters claim to have seen, for instance, the kind that Whitley Strieber recounts having met in his controversial bestseller *Communion* (1987). Their most extraordinary power is that they can only be remembered when they are seen, so they have been able to persist on Earth for many years almost unknown by humans, or, rather, only known as a vague rumour or legend.

There's an obvious similarity here with the *Weeping Angels* (Chapter 2). Both were created by Steven Moffat, and both have an existence that depends on the gaze of others. One might start to worry that this is a signal that Moffat only has a finite number of great *Doctor Who* ideas, but this story certainly contains enough ideas to keep the viewer happy. The Doctor's eventual solution to the Silence's presence on Earth is to work against this most extraordinary trait of the monsters. He inserts a few seconds of footage of a Silent into the film of the Apollo Moon landing. Therefore, every time a human sees that footage, they'll be reminded of the aliens' presence on the planet, and the need to overthrow them.

So the Silents, like so many of Moffat's creations, are designed very deliberately to scare children. Moreover, they're clearly designed to do so in an interactive way. Just as the last montage of *Blink* encouraged children to think that statues around them might be Weeping Angels trapped into immobility, so everything about the Silents is designed with a kind of game in mind. A child might have seen one, and would have forgotten it, until it cropped up in, say, their dreams. It is possible to believe that the Silents might be real. They are, as the intelligence fraternity say, *deniable*.

The Silents haunt the rest of the 2011 season, though they only make a further appearance in the finale, *The Wedding of River Song.* It becomes clear that they are only part of a larger consortium dedicated to killing the Doctor. To this end, they have bred River Song, the child of his companions Amy and Rory, to kill him. The Doctor bluffs an escape to his assassination at the end of the season, as he realises that the Silence that's being required is his own. He has become too well-known, too much of a myth. So he creates the impression that he has indeed died, and vanishes into the shadows. Clearly, there is much more about the Silence that we have yet to find out. They are, it's clear, dedicated to stopping the Doctor answering 'the oldest question': 'Doctor Who?' The question of who the Doctor really is has been carefully unanswered for the whole of the series' life. If I was asked to place a bet, I'd suggest that the series is headed towards some kind of reboot or reset at its 50th anniversary, in 2013. I have, of course, no inside information, but it would be appropriate if the Silents were a part of this. The Doctor is, especially, in his most recent incarnations, an incessant talker. For such a character, silence would be a death sentence.

What can be said at the moment is that the 2011 season is, to use corporate language, one in which the Doctor decides to undertake a major repositioning of his brand. The Silents have played a central part in this, and it's by no means clear that their role is finished.

CONCLUSION

I said at the start of this book that my definition of a monster was a race of creatures that was nonhuman and evil. Hence some of the well-known creatures in *Doctor Who* I have not discussed. The Master, for instance, is unarguably evil, but basically human most of the time. The Draconians, in *Frontier in Space* (1973), are nonhuman but well-intentioned. I admit that I've stretched these definitions at times; the Ice Warriors are, as I argued in Chapter 25, depicted as being more than capable of good behaviour. The Adipose aren't inherently evil (although their breeding does cause others to die), nor are the Silurians and Sea Devils (though they choose evil actions in most of their stories). This, as my comments in the last chapter suggested, is one of the questions that interests me most about the field: How much do monsters have a choice about being monstrous, and how much they can outgrow their natures?

Before getting to that question, though, it may be worth thinking about some rough categories of creatures considered in this book. The basic function of any monster, from a story point of view, is to look scary and create jeopardy. But, because the series is called *Doctor Who* rather than, say, *The Toclafane*, it must be resolvable jeopardy. There must be a way to defeat these creatures and restore normality. Often, as I've suggested, the source of a monster's defeat may be something inherent in its own nature. All of this would apply to a creature that's conceptually quite simple, such as Kroll, as well as more complex ones such as the Weeping Angels.

One distinction, actually quite a fundamental one, is between monsters that are capable of speech and those that are not. Those that are not tend to be more *elemental* threats; they cannot be reasoned with. Of course, creatures that do not speak are perfectly capable of communicating in other ways.

Having made these distinctions, it seems to me that the creatures I've discussed in this book fall into a couple of broad categories. First, there are a set of them that are, in one way or another, warnings about science overreaching itself, or having insufficient regard for the consequences of its actions. This would include the Borad, the Primords and the Haemovores. The Cybermen probably fall into this category, at least when they have been taken close to their original concept of humans whose failing organs have been replaced by mechanical implants, as they are in *The Tenth Planet* and *Rise of the Cybermen/The Age of Steel*. In other stories, such as *The Moonbase* or *Revenge of the Cybermen*, they are far closer to being generic evil robots.

A second category of monsters includes those that are depicted as being inherently warlike. The prime example here is the Sontarans, whose nature is fixed by their cloned genetic template. The Ice Warriors and the Sycorax probably also belong in this category, as to an extent do the Daleks. The difference with the Daleks is that they do not glory in war per se; they do not elevate deeds of bravery like the Sontarans and the Ice Warriors. Instead, war is the necessary and inevitable consequence of their mission to become the sole life form in creation.

A third category is what might be called the predators. These are often, though not always, creatures without speech. I'm thinking of creatures such as Kroll, the Weeping Angels, the Mandrels and the Cheetah-people. Many of these might, in a sense, be excused from the accusation of being evil because they are just pursuing their nature, and their lack of sentience gives them no choice in the matter.

A fourth category, although quite a varied one, is what might be called the rationalised myth. This would certainly include the Dæmons, the Mara and the Fendahl, as well as some creatures I've not had the chance to discuss in detail such as the Nimon. The central characteristic here is that the creature is something previously talked about in stories and myths, which Doctor Who then rationalises and places into its science fiction frame. It doesn't much matter whether the myth is one that viewers might already be aware of (as with the Dæmons), or one that's partly or wholly invented (as with the Fendahl).

Having created those rough categories, there are a few creatures that don't easily fit into any of them. The Axons might, I suppose, be thought of as predators (all the more when the original title of their story, *The Vampire from Space*), but they feel too intelligent and manipulative to sit with the others in that category. The Zarbi might sit in the category of predators, but they really deserve to be considered along with the rest of the ecosystem of Vortis, Menoptra and all. The single greatest exception to this categorisation, though, is the Silurian/Sea Devil race. Although their civilisation is barely glimpsed, the whole point about them is that they are not monsters. Despite their strange appearance, they are an alternative set of inhabitants of Earth, as strange to us as we are to them.

It's also striking, considering the list of monsters in the Glossary, how few are genuinely original. So many monsters take the lead, in their conception or design or both, from existing creatures or concepts. The Sea Devils are clearly based on turtles, the Cheetah-people on cats, the Autons on shop-window dummies and so on. This is leaving aside a story like *Planet of the Spiders* (1974), whose monsters are, simply, giant intelligent versions of the spiders we know here on Earth. In a sense, using an existing concept as the basis for a monster makes things easier for the programme-makers. A giant spider, for instance, plays on common fears of the real thing, and also allows a degree of clarity about what exactly the creature is. As I said at the start of this book, there's an argument that the most-remembered monsters in all Doctor Who's history are the giant maggots from *The Green Death*.

This isn't a criticism, though, nor should it be too surprising. *Doctor Who* has always been a programme that has drawn from other sources, whether in its monsters or otherwise. (As an example, consider the passages in the revised editions of *The Writer's Tale* in which Russell T Davies frankly acknowledges the debt of *The End of Time* (2009–10) to *Harry Potter*, *The Matrix*, and *Being John Malkovich*.) In a sense, one of the programme's functions is to introduce these stories or tropes to a younger audience who might not yet have encountered them. So one might imagine them going on from one of the programme's vampire stories to a source-text like *Dracula*. In its monsters, as in its stories, the show is a kind of attractor, pulling in tropes from outside and transforming them into *Doctor Who*-ness. *Doctor Who*, like so many of its monsters, is an omnivore.

GLOSSARY

Although this book does not aim to be comprehensive in its coverage of monsters, I provide here a reasonably full alphabetical listing of creatures to have appeared in the series to date, cross-referenced to chapters in this book where appropriate. Cross-references to other entries are indicated by a change in font, thus: **Daleks**.

Abzorbaloff Chameleon creature that survives by absorbing, on touch, the essences of others; featured in *Love and Monsters* (2006).

Adipose Small creatures 'liberated' from human fat by the process pioneered by Adipose Industries in *Partners in Crime* (2008); see Chapter 24.

Androgums Humanoid creatures with a pronounced interest in food and cooking, encountered in *The Two Doctors* (1985).

Atraxi Unseen aliens fulfilling the role of police/prison warders in *The Eleventh Hour* (2010).

Autons Animate plastic mannequins in the service of the Nestene Consciousness, encountered in *Spearhead from Space* (1970), *Terror of the Autons* (1971) and *Rose* (2005), and discussed in Chapter 1.

Axons Manifestations of the entity known as Axos, manifesting both as golden-skinned humanoids and tentacled creatures in *The Claws of Axos* (1971); see Chapter 6.

Bandrils Aliens from a neighbouring planet to Karfel in *Timelash* (1985); an attack by them on Karfel is provoked by the **Borad** and prevented by the Doctor.

Borad Assumed name of a scientist and leader of the planet Karfel after he became deformed as a result of experimentation on the **Morlox** in *Timelash* (1985); see Chapter 5.

Carrionites Race of witch-like creatures encountered in *The Shakespeare Code* (2007), supposedly inspirations behind the witches in Shakespeare's *Macbeth*.

Cat-people The unnamed race that supplies the cat-nun/nurses from *New Earth* (2006) and a range of other characters in *Gridlock* (2007). Seemingly unrelated to the **Cheetah-people**.

Chameleons The eponymous aliens in *The Faceless Ones*+ (1967), who attempt to steal the identities of humans.

Cheetah-people Inhabitants of an unnamed planet in *Survival* (1989), who are able to teleport to Earth and abduct humans; see Chapter 28.

Chimerons Alien race almost wiped out prior to the events of *Delta and the Bannermen*; the Doctor helps their last surviving member, fallen by accident to Earth in 1959, to hatch the egg she has brought with her and continue the species.

Cryons Humanoid creatures inhabiting the tombs of the **Cybermen** on the planet Telos in *Attack of the Cybermen* (1985); they are only able to survive in conditions of extreme cold.

Cybermen Cybernetic creatures created by a human-like race progressively replacing their organic bodies with mechanical components so as to drive out all emotion. Original accounts of their creation described them as coming from the planet Mondas, a twin of the Earth, but subsequent stories described their home as Telos. In the post-2005 series, they have a further origin story, being created in a parallel Earth by a terminally ill scientist. They make substantive appearances in *The Tenth Planet*+ (1966), *The Moonbase*+ (1967), *The Tomb of the Cybermen* (1967), *The Wheel in Space*+ (1968), *The Invasion*+ (1968), *Revenge of the Cybermen* (1975), *Earthshock* (1982), *The Five Doctors*

(1983), *Attack of the Cybermen* (1985), *Silver Nemesis* (1988), *Rise of the Cybermen/The Age of Steel* (2006), *Army of Ghosts/Doomsday* (2006), *The Next Doctor* (2008) and *Closing Time* (2011). They are discussed in Chapters 8, 19 and 23.

Dæmons Extremely powerful aliens who influenced Earth's development, and so were remembered as myths in its history. One was encountered in *The Daemons* (1971); see Chapter 17.

Daleks Name given to the machines containing the mutated remains of the Kaled race. The machines were originally invented by the Kaled scientist Davros. Their appeal to *Doctor Who*'s audience was immediate, and they have become the show's most revisited monster. The Daleks have made substantive appearances in *The Daleks* (1963–64), *The Dalek Invasion of Earth* (1964), *The Chase* (1965), *Mission to the Unknown+* (1965), *The Daleks' Master Plan+* (1965–66), *The Power of the Daleks+* (1966), *The Evil of the Daleks+* (1967), *Day of the Daleks* (1972), *Planet of the Daleks* (1973), *Death to the Daleks* (1974), *Genesis of the Daleks* (1975), *Destiny of the Daleks* (1979), *The Five Doctors* (1983), *Resurrection of the Daleks* (1984), *Revelation of the Daleks* (1985), *Remembrance of the Daleks* (1988), *Dalek* (2005), *Bad Wolf/The Parting of the Ways* (2005), *Army of Ghosts/Doomsday* (2006), *Daleks in Manhattan/Evolution of the Daleks* (2007), *The Stolen Earth/Journey's End* (2008), *The Waters of Mars* (2009) and *Victory of the Daleks* (2010). They are discussed in Chapters 7, 13, 16 and 32.

Destroyer Devil-like creature unleashed by the witch Morgaine in *Battlefield* (1989).

Draconians A civilised race with a huge empire whose interests come into conflict with humanity's in *Frontier in Space* (1973).

Drashigs Huge, stupid and ferocious reptilian creatures, encountered in miniaturised form in *Carnival of Monsters* (1972).

Eight Legs A race of mutated and enlarged spiders found on the planet Metebelis 3 in *Planet of the Spiders* (1974).

Ergon Bird-like servant of the renegade Time Lord Omega in *Arc of Infinity* (1983).

Foamasi Intelligent reptilian creatures who fought a hugely destructive war against the humanoid Argolins many years before the events depicted in *The Leisure Hive* (1980).

Fendahl A gestalt entity whose attempted resurrection is depicted in *Image of the Fendahl* (1977). Its components appeared to be worm-like creatures, but led by a golden-skinned woman; see Chapter 29.

Fish People Aquatic servants of the people of Atlantis in *The Underwater Menace+* (1967).

Gangers Technologically-created doppelgangers of humans in *The Rebel Flesh/The Almost People* (2011).

Gel Guards Blobby servants of the renegade Time Lord Omega in *The Three Doctors* (1973).

Gelth Gaseous creatures, refugees from the Time War, encountered in *The Unquiet Dead* (2005).

Haemovores Vampire-like products of a future polluted Earth, encountered in *The Curse of Fenric* (1989); see Chapter 12.

Hath Land-based but fish-like creatures locked in a war on the planet Messaline in *The Doctor's Daughter* (2008).

Ice Warriors Reptilian inhabitants of Mars who appeared in earlier stories to be purely interested in conquest, but who later became more nuanced figures. They appeared in *The Ice Warriors+* (1967), *The Seeds of Death* (1969), *The Curse of Peladon* (1972) and *The Monster of Peladon* (1974) and are discussed in Chapter 25.

Isolus Tiny alien which befriends the lonely girl Chloe in *Fear Her* (2006).

Jagaroth Warlike humanoid creatures with one eye; the last of their kind, Scaroth, is encountered in *City of Death* (1979).

Jacondans Bird-like inhabitants of the planet Jaconda in *The Twin Dilemma* (1984).

Jagrafess Huge, vicious, gelatinous creature residing on, and controlling the news output of, Satellite Five in *The Long Game* (2005).

Judoon Rhinoceros-like galactic police who first appeared in *Smith and Jones* (2007) and returned in *The Stolen Earth* (2008).

Kastrians Silicon-based (and crystalline) creatures whose civilisation was destroyed by Eldrad, the villain of *The Hand of Fear* (1976).

Kraals Grumpy, rhinoceros-like aliens who attempt to conquer Earth in *The Android Invasion* (1975).

Krafayis Fierce and invisible creature encountered in *Vincent and the Doctor* (2010).

Krillitanes Chameleon race infesting the school, and controlling the pupils, in *School Reunion* (2006).

Kroll Octopoid creature grown to great size because of the influence of the fifth segment of the Key to Time in *The Power of Kroll* (1979); See Chapter 3.

Krotons Crystalline aliens who enslave the peaceful Gonds in *The Krotons* (1969) until the Doctor's arrival.

Krynoids Plant-like creature, travelling as pairs of seeds, and seen in *The Seeds of Doom* (1976) to grow to immense size after possessing a human host.

Lurmans Grey (in character and appearance) inhabitants of Inter Minor, whose life is disrupted by the arrival of the showman Vorg and his Miniscope containing **Drashigs** in *Carnival of Monsters* (1972).

Macra Crablike aliens first seen terrorising a holiday planet in *The Macra Terror+* (1967), and encountered again, after evolutionary regression, in *Gridlock* (2007).

Malus Manifestation of a warlike alien creature, as a medieval image of the Devil, as it appeared in the Earth village of Little Hodcombe in *The Awakening* (1984).

Mandrels Ferocious, green-eyed creatures which transform into the drug vraxoin on their death; see *The Nightmare of Eden* (1979), and Chapter 30.

Mara Snake-like creature first encountered among the aboriginal people of Deva Loka in Kinda (1982) and subsequently on its home planet of Manussa in Snakedance (1983); see Chapter 31.

Marshmen Swamp-dwelling creatures who are another form of the 'humans' encountered in *Full Circle* (1980); see Chapter 20.

"Martians" The eponymous aliens in *The Ambassadors of Death*; see Chapter 26.

Mechanoids Spherical robots whose rivalry and battle with the Daleks forms the climax of *The Chase* (1965).

Menoptra Intelligent butterfly-like creatures who form an alliance with the Doctor in *The Web Planet* (1965); see Chapter 14.

Mentors A green amphibious race, first encountered in the person of their greedy representative Sil in *Vengeance on Varos* (1985). Sil returns, along with other members of the species, in the 'Mindwarp' section (Episodes 5–8) of *The Trial of a Time Lord* (1986), set on their home planet of Thoros Beta.

Monoids One-eyed humanoid race originally encountered as servants of humanity in *The Ark* (1966) and subsequently (after a break of several hundred years in the story) their brutal masters.

Morlox Savage cave-dwelling creatures encountered in *Timelash* (1985).

Nimon Bull like creatures, explicitly based on the mythological Minotaur, featured in *The Horns of Nimon* (1979–80).

Ogri Mobile silicon creatures, disguised as part of an English stone circle and fed on blood in *The Stones of Blood* (1978).

Ogrons Huge, primitive creatures who act as servants of the Daleks in *Day of the Daleks* and *Frontier in Space*.

Ood Race of servant-creatures in *The Impossible Planet/The Satan Pit* (2006), whose nature is explored further in *Planet of the Ood* (2008) and *The End of Time* (2009–10); see Chapter 21.

Osirans Extremely powerful aliens, all but vanished from the universe in our time; *Pyramids of Mars* (1975) concerns the Doctor's battle with the last of them, Sutekh.

Primords Humans infected by the slime created during the 'Inferno' drilling project became transformed into these bestial creatures in *Inferno* (1970); see Chapter 4.

Pyroviles Creatures of fire and rock shown to be behind the eruption of Mount Vesuvius in *The Fires of Pompeii* (2008).

Quarks Small robot servants employed by the eponymous conquerors in *The Dominators* (1968).

Racnoss Race of giant spider creatures whose Empress is encountered in *The Runaway Bride* (2006).

Raston Robot Silver humanoid creature with astonishing efficiency in killing, as demonstrated in *The Five Doctors* (1983).

Reapers The winged creatures (not named onscreen) who emerge to swarm around the 'wound' in time created in *Father's Day* (2005).

Rills An ugly and benign reptilian race seen in *Galaxy Four*+ (1965) and discussed in Chapter 5.

Rutans Jellyfish-like creatures locked in an endless war with the Sontarans. Their only appearance was in *Horror of Fang Rock* (1977).

Sea Devils Submarine cousins of the **Silurians**, encountered in *The Sea Devils* (1972) and then in *Warriors of the Deep* (1984); see Chapter 11.

Sensorites Telepathic race with bulbous heads, originating on the planet Sense-Sphere, who made their only appearance in *The Sensorites* (1964).

Silurians Reptilian predecessors of humanity who were forced into hibernation millions of years ago by an oncoming catastrophe and who re-emerge in the twentieth century. They made their original appearance in *Doctor Who and the Silurians* (1970), and returned, along with their cousins the **Sea Devils**, in *Warriors of the Deep* (1984). A further appearance by the Silurians alone occurred in *The Hungry Earth/Cold Blood* (2010), with a cameo in *A Good Man Goes To War* (2011). They are discussed in Chapter 11.

Silents Humanoid aliens who are only remembered when they are seen, who make appearances in *The Impossible Astronaut/Day of the Moon* (2011) and *The Wedding of River Song* (2011); see Chapter 33.

Slitheen Family of criminals/scrap merchants from the planet Raxacoricofallapatorius, first encountered in *Aliens of London/World War Three* (2005), and one of whom survives to *Boom Town* (2005); see Chapter 10.

Solonians Natives of the planet Solos, whose elaborate life-cycle is a subject of *The Mutants* (1972).

Sontarans A militaristic cloned race locked in a perpetual war with the **Rutans**. They appear in *The Time Warrior* (1973–74), *The Sontaran Experiment* (1975), *The Invasion of Time* (1978), *The Two Doctors* (1985), *The Sontaran Stratagem/ The Poison Sky* (2008) and *The End of Time* (2009–10), along with a cameo in *A Good Man Goes To War* (2011) and they are discussed in Chapter 9.

Sycorax Bone-masked invaders of Earth repelled by the Doctor in *The Christmas Invasion* (2005); see Chapter 18.

Terileptils Intelligent and civilised reptilian creatures, apparently named from a contraction of 'territorial reptile'; three criminals of this race are shown as fugitives on seventeenth-century Earth in *The Visitation* (1982).

Tetraps Bat-like creatures used by the renegade Time Lord the Rani as part of her plans on the planet Lakertya in *Time and the Rani* (1987).

Tharils Leonine creatures shown as enslaved by humans in *Warrior's Gate* (1981), but who were previously the masters; see Chapter 22.

Toclafane Spherical metal creatures containing the remains of humanity from the end of the universe's life; their creation is prefigured in *Utopia* (2007) and they are then featured in *The Sound of Drums/Last of the Time Lords* (2007); see Chapter 27.

Tractators Burrowing creatures who are able to exert gravitational force to bring down meteors on the human colony in *Frontios* (1984).

Tree-people Race encountered by the Doctor and Rose as guests at the party to mark the Earth's destruction in *The End of the World* (2005).

Tythonians Huge, pale, globular creatures – Erato, encountered in *The Creature from the Pit* (1979) is the only one featured in the series to far.

Urbankans Frog-like creatures, whose representatives had visited Earth, and taken away samples of its cultures, at various points before the events depicted in *Four to Doomsday* (1982).

Vashta Nerada Creatures manifesting as moving shadows who feed on human flesh in *Silence in the Library/Forest of the Dead* (2008).

Vervoids Plant-like creatures who cause mayhem on the spaceship Hyperion 3 in the third section (Episodes 9–12, 'Terror of the Vervoids') of *The Trial of a Time Lord* (1986).

Vespiform The true wasp-like form of the murderer in *The Unicorn and the Wasp* (2008).

Vinvocci Green, cactus-like aliens who help the Doctor in *The End of Time* (2009–10), related to the **Zocci**.

Voord Black-skinned creatures who made their only appearance in *The Keys of Marinus* (1964), attempting to obtain the eponymous keys.

War Machines Tank-like robots created by a megalomaniac computer in *The War Machines* (1966); at the computer's bidding, they wreak havoc in contemporary London.

Weed creature An otherwise unnamed sea organism in *Fury from the Deep*+ (1968) which appears to be a semi-sentient seaweed-like parasite, and vulnerable to high-pitched sounds.

Weeping Angels Creatures with the appearance of statues in *Blink* (2007) and *The Time of Angels/Flesh and Stone* (2010). They are 'quantum-locked' so that they cannot move while being observed, and they are discussed in Chapter 2.

The Wire Parasitic creature dwelling within the televisions in *The Idiot's Lantern* (2006).

Wirrn Spacefaring insect-like race whose life-cycle, parasitic upon human hosts, is shown in *The Ark in Space* (1975) and discussed in Chapter 15.

Xeraphin Gestalt creature, presenting as a 'good' and an 'evil' persona, whose power has been coerced into service by The Master, in *Time-Flight* (1982).

Yeti Robot servants of the astral 'Great Intelligence' in *The Abominable Snowmen*+ (1967) and *The Web of Fear*+ (1968), designed to look like the Himalayan monsters of legend. They made a cameo return in *The Five Doctors* (1983).

Zarbi Ant-like creatures native to the planet Vortis, as shown in *The Web Planet* (1965), and discussed in Chapter 14.

Zocci Small, red, cactus-like aliens (and related to the **Vinvocci**), one of whom is Bannakaffalatta, seen in *Voyage of the Damned* (2007).

Zygons Aliens with a shape-shifting ability encountered in *Terror of the Zygons* (1975).

REFERENCES

The Ascent of Man (1973) Dir Adrian Malone BBC, London.

La Belle et La Bête (1946) Dir Jean Cocteau, Discina.

Bettelheim, Bruno (1976) *The Uses of Enchantment: The Meaning and Importance of Fairy-Tales.* Knopf, New York.

Bidmead, Christopher H (1981) *Doctor Who: Logopolis.* Target, London.

Bailey, D (2008) 'Script Doctors' interview with Steven Moffat. In *Doctor Who Magazine* 394, 30 April 2008, pp 46–50.

Bhabha, Homi (1994) *The Location of Culture.* Routledge, London and New York.

Bradshaw, Simon, Keen, Anthony and Sleight, Graham, eds (2011) *The Unsilent Library: Essays on the Russell T Davies Era of new Doctor Who.* Science Fiction Foundation, London.

Butler, D (ed) (2007) *Time and Relative Dissertations in Space.* Manchester University Press, Manchester.

Card, Orson Scott (1986) *Speaker for the Dead.* Tor, New York.

Cartmel, Andrew (2005) *Script Doctor: The Inside Story of Doctor Who 1986–89.* Reynolds and Hearn, London.

Clarke, Arthur C (1953) *Childhood's End.* Ballantine, New York.

Clute, John (1995) *Look at the Evidence: Essays and Reviews.* Liverpool University Press, Liverpool.

Clute, John and Nicholls, Peter (eds) (1993) *The Encyclopedia of Science Fiction.* Orbit, London.

Clute, John and Grant, John (1997) *The Encyclopedia of Fantasy.* Orbit, London.

Cook, Benjamin (2005a) 'Tooth and Claw: The Russell T Davies interview'. In *Doctor Who Magazine* 360, 14 September 2005, pp. 12–19.

Cook, B (2005b) 'The Christmas Invasion Preview'. In *Doctor Who Magazine* 364, December 2005, pp. 22–23.

Cook, B (2007) Preview for *Blink*. In *Doctor Who Magazine* 383, 27 June 2007, p. 21.

Crowley, John (1976) *Beasts*. Doubleday, Garden City, NY.

Davies, R T et al. (2005) *Doctor Who: The Shooting Scripts*. BBC Books, London.

Davies, Russell T and Cook, Benjamin (2008) *Doctor Who: The Writer's Tale,* BBC Books, London.

Datlow, Ellen (ed) (1989) *Blood is not Enough: 17 stories of Vampirism,* William Morrow, New York.

The Devil Rides Out (1968) Dir Terence Fisher, Hammer.

Doctor Who and the Daleks (1965) Dir David Yates, Gordon Flemyng, Amicus.

Graves, Robert (1955) *The Greek Myths*. (2 vols) Penguin, Harmondsworth.

Harrison, Harry (1966) *Make Room! Make Room!* Doubleday, Garden City, NY.

Hills, Matt (2010) *Triumph of a Time Lord: Regenerating Doctor Who for the 21st Century*. I.B.Tauris, London.

Hodges, Andrew (1983) *Alan Turing: The Enigma*. Burnett Books, London.

Howe, David J (1997) *Doctor Who: Monsters*. BBC Books, London.

Howe, David J and Walker, Stephen James (1998) *Doctor Who: The Television Companion*. BBC Books, London.

Hulke, Malcolm (1974) *Doctor Who and the Cave Monsters*. W H Allen, London.

Lewontin, R C (2001) *The Doctrine of DNA*. Penguin, London.

Lofficer, Jean-Marc and Lofficer, Randy (1997) *The Nth Doctor: An in-depth study of the films that almost were*. Virgin Publishing, London.

MacLeod, Ken (2005) *Learning the World: A Novel of First Contact*. Orbit, London.

Miles, L and T Wood (2004a) *About Time: The Unauthorized Guide to Doctor Who. 1970–1974: Seasons 7 to 11*. Mad Norwegian Press, New Orleans, LA.

Miles, L and T Wood (2004b) *About Time: The Unauthorized Guide to Doctor Who. 1975–1979: Seasons 12 to 17*. Mad Norwegian Press, New Orleans, LA.

Miles, L and T Wood (2005) *About Time: The Unauthorized Guide to Doctor Who. 1980–1984: Seasons 18 to 21*. Mad Norwegian Press, New Orleans, LA.

Moore, C L (1944) 'No Woman Born' *Astounding Science Fiction*.

Pinker, Steven (1994) *The Language Instinct*. HarperCollins, New York.

Pixley, A (2005) *The Doctor Who Companion: Series One* (ed C Hickman). Tunbridge Wells: Panini Comics.

Russ, Joanna (2007) *The Country You Have Never Seen: Essays and Reviews*. Liverpool University Press, Liverpool.

The Second Coming (2003) Dir Adrian Shergold, ITV.

Shearman, Robert (2003) *Jubilee*. Big Finish, London.

Sheckley, Robert (1952) 'The Leech', *Galaxy Science Fiction*, December 1952.

Sleight, Graham (2006) 'Distraction' In *The Arthur C. Clarke Award, A Critical Anthology*, (ed Paul Kincaid), Serendip Foundation, Northampton.

Soylent Green (1973) Dir Richard Fleischer, MGM.

Stoker, Bram (1897) *Dracula*. Constable, London.

Strieber, Whitley (1987) *Communion: A True Story*. Avon, New York,

Tiptree, James Jr (1988) *The Color of Neanderthal Eyes*. Tor Doubles, New York.

Tolkien, JRR (1936) 'Beowulf: The Monsters and the Critics'. *Proceedings of the British Academy*, 22 (1936), pp. 245–95

Tulloch, John and Jenkins, Henry (1995) *Science Fiction Audiences: Watching* Doctor Who *and* Star Trek. Routledge, London and New York.

Tulloch, John and Alvarado, Manuel (1983) *Doctor Who: The Unfolding Text*. Macmillan, London.

Turner, Alwyn (2011) *The Man Who Invented the Daleks*. Aurum Press, London.

Waugh, Evelyn (1948) *The Loved One*. London, Chapman & Hall.

Wood, T and L Miles (2006a) *About Time: The Unauthorized Guide to Doctor Who. 1963–1966: Seasons 1 to 3*. Mad Norwegian Press, Des Moines, IA.

Wood, T and L Miles (2006b) *About Time: The Unauthorized Guide to Doctor Who. 1966–1969: Seasons 4 to 6*. Mad Norwegian Press, Des Moines, IA.

Wood, T (2007) *About Time: The Unauthorized Guide to Doctor Who. 1985–1989: Seasons 22 to 26, The TV Movie*. Mad Norwegian Press, Des Moines, IA.

INDEX